Restorative Justice and Criminal Justice

Exploring the Relationship

Edited by Linda Gröning and Jørn Jacobsen

Santérus
Academic Press
Sweden

www.santerus.se

© 2012 The authors and Santérus Academic Press Sweden
ISBN 978-91-7335-032-7
Editing: Clifford Owen, Polished Texts
Cover illustration: Painterly Architectonic by Lyubov Popova 1918.
Cover profile: Sven Bylander
Santérus Academic Press is an imprint of
Santérus Förlag, Stockholm, Sweden
academicpress@santerus.se
www.santerus.se
Printed by BOD, Germany 2012

Contents

Acknowledgements   7

LINDA GRÖNING, & JØRN JACOBSEN
1. Introduction:
   Restorative justice and the criminal justice system   9

DAVID C. VOGT
2. The aims of restorative justice: Some philosophical remarks on
   the challenges of integrating restorative justice into the criminal
   justice system. Reconciling the irreconcilable?   21

KATJA JANSEN FREDRIKSEN & EIRIK HOVDEN
3. Restorative justice in Islamic criminal law?   41

HENDRIK KAPTEIN
4. Victims of inconclusive criminal evidence against offenders:
   State liability and some more restorative semi-remedies   61

INGUN FORNES
5. Restorative justice in the Norwegian juvenile justice system   93

ELIZABETH BAUMANN
6. Striking a balance between justice and peace:
   Restorative justice in states of transition   123

List of Contributors   177

Acknowledgements

The majority of the articles in this anthology stem from a symposium that was held in Bergen in 2010. The initiative arose within a current research project, *Criminal Law Theory: A New Norwegian Approach*. This project seeks to address fruitful approaches to the criminal law in order to stimulate new discussions that give us a broader understanding of criminal law. Doing this work, it became clear to us that several among the staff at the Faculty of Law in Bergen were occupied with the discussion about restorative justice in their own research. This led to a symposium in which these perspectives were presented and exchanged – followed by a stimulating discussion. We found the perspectives so enriching that we wanted to share them by means of this book.

The editors of this book would like to thank the contributors for the good co-operation at the symposium and the insights delivered by the engaging discussions in its aftermath and also in the creation of the articles. The editors also wish to give special thanks to senior lecturer Hendrik Kaptein, who entered the process at a later stage and generously both commented on the other articles as well as provided us with an article of his own as a valuable contribution to this project. The editors also wish to thank the other participants at the symposium for their contribution to the stimulating discussions. Thanks in particular also to Professor Jørn Øyrehagen Sunde for his extensive contribution to this project. We also thank Torbjörn Santérus at Santérus Publishing for publishing the book and Esbjörn Kleist for his work in this process.

The book has been made possible by a generous funding from the Faculty of Law, University of Bergen.

Bergen, 30 January 2012

Linda Gröning and Jørn Jacobsen

1. Introduction: Restorative justice and the criminal justice system

LINDA GRÖNING, & JØRN JACOBSEN

1.1 The aim of the book

This book is concerned with restorative justice and criminal justice. More specifically, its focus is on exploring restorative justice with regard to ideas, rules and system structures connected to the traditional Western model of a criminal justice system, including the conventional criminal process. As a starting point, it seems clear that the perspectives of restorative justice challenge this model. As an alternative to traditional ideas, the current restorative justice movement raises questions about the potential for replacing traditional structure, and processes of criminal justice with programmes or processes of restorative justice. This book does not aspire to answer these wide-ranging questions directly. Instead it aims to explore the relationship between restorative justice and criminal justice from a variety of different perspectives. By doing so, the aim of the book is to articulate different ideas of what restorative justice is and its relationship to the traditional criminal justice system.

1.2 The reference point: The traditional understanding of a criminal justice system

In order to provide a better understanding of the departure point and context of this book, and more generally of the (still) dominant perspectives of criminal law, it seems necessary first to clarify what we refer to by the term traditional model of criminal justice, and the system aimed at realising it. Despite some apparent differences, the Western criminal justice systems to a large extent have common traits. In this respect, the paradigm of the national criminal justice system corresponds to some basic ideas about what a criminal justice system is and how it should function as a system. These ideas are so firmly anchored in Western legal discourse that they – in spite of all controversial details – can be said to form a traditional model of a criminal justice system.[1]

In brief, the traditional model is centred on the idea that the criminal justice system is the state's legal apparatus for the use of public penal power. The purpose of the criminal justice system is to secure social order on the territory of the state, by means of crime control through the threat and use of punishment. From this starting point, the basic justification for the system's existence lies, paradigmatically, in the argument of general deterrence. At the same time the criminal justice system should secure criminal justice. In this respect, the criminal justice system is typically considered as rooted in the basic values of the democratic *Rechtsstaat*,[2] of individual autonomy, equality and in the desire to avoid the abuse of power (both from public institutions and from other individuals). In other words, the criminal justice system aims at both effective crime prevention and effective prevention of the abuse of public penal power.

As the overall legal system of the state, the criminal justice system is most often taken to include, as a minimum, both a certain system of norms and a certain organisation of institutions authorised with different kinds of competencies of public power. As basic elements of the criminal justice system, the system of norms contains both

1   See further Linda Gröning, 'A Criminal Justice System or a System Deficit: Notes on the System Structure of the EU Criminal Law', *European Journal of Crime, Criminal Law and Criminal Justice*, 18 (2010), pp. 115–137.

2   A *Rechtsstaat* is defined here as a state in which the authorities are allowed to intervene in the legal position of individual citizens only on the basis of law, not by armed force or at the authorities' own discretion. A *Rechtsstaat* is furthermore a State in which the authorities themselves are bound by the rules that they have created and from which they cannot deviate at their own discretion. Deviation and exception from the rules can be allowed only in a way that is prescribed by law. In a *Rechtsstaat* legal security is a fundamental principle. Many will also presume that a *Rechtsstaat* respects fundamental human rights. See further Jørn Jacobsen: *Fragment til forståing av den rettsstatlege strafferetten* (Bergen, 2009), ch. 3, Fagbokforlaget.

rules of substantive criminal law and rules of criminal procedure. The substantive rules define the crimes that are to be punished in the particular state or country and are in this respect at the centre of the criminal justice system. These rules are paradigmatically divided into a general and a special part. In addition, the rules of substantive criminal law are most often taken to protect the most fundamental interests of a certain (national) society. The rules of procedure determine how the state enforces the substantive rules of the criminal law by assessing the occurrence of crime and convicting and punishing those responsible for the crime. At the core of the traditional view of criminal justice lies in particular this view that it is the state that is exclusively responsible for the administration of criminal justice, which means, *inter alia*, that the victim is not part of the process.[3]

On a deeper legal theoretical level, the system of norms of the criminal justice system, in particular the rules of substantive criminal law, is typically understood as a monistic system of rules (founded in one constitutional source only) that is internally consistent and coherent and that consists of a hierarchical structure with mechanisms for resolving legal inconsistency. In more general terms, the traditional model rests upon the idea of the rule of law, at least in its formal sense (*cf.* legality). The basic requirement of legal certainty is at the core of the criminal justice system.

Regarding its institutional organisation, the criminal justice system is typically a system with a certain separation of powers, consisting primarily of three levels – where a certain kind of power is exercised by certain authorities on each level. These levels are the 'level of legislation (or criminalisation)', the 'level of adjudication of guilt and punishment' and the 'level of administration of punishment'. On these levels, legislators, courts and administrative authorities respectively exercise different powers.[4] In addition there are other important actors that are attached to the functioning of the criminal justice system (primarily to the level of adjudication of guilt and punishment), such as the police, the prosecutors and the defence.

As a state-based system, the criminal justice system is viewed as

---

3   See, *inter alia*, A. Ashworth and M. Redmayne, *The Criminal Process*, 4th edition (New York: Oxford University Press, 2010), p. 54.

4   See N. Jareborg, *Straffrättsideologiska fragment* (Uppsala: Iustus, 1992) pp. 136–137.

subordinated to the basic requirements of legitimacy of the demo-cratic *Rechtsstaat*,[5] above all the criteria of democratic legitimacy and protection of individual rights.

At the same time as the national criminal justice system is con-sidered a subsystem of the legal order of the state, it is also consid-ered a particular system with an idiosyncratic 'grammar of criminal law', which is centred on the notions of crime and punishment and which embodies principles and concepts that distinguish the crimi-nal law from other branches of law. In this respect, the principle of guilt and the closely connected idea of penal censure (*i.e.*, the idea that punishment expresses moral blame; crime as wrongdoing), the principle of *ultima ratio* (*i.e.*, the principle that criminalisation should be used as last resort) and the principle of proportionality (between crime and punishment) are all principles that often are underlined as distinguishing features of the criminal justice system.

1.3　Introducing an alternative: The restorative justice approach

Restorative justice, as understood in the contemporary debate, in essence signifies a process in which offenders, victims, their repre-sentatives and representatives of the community come together to agree on a response to a crime. Through the multitude of different restorative justice processes – such as victim–offender mediation, sentencing circles or restorative cautioning schemes – perspec-tives of restorative justice often underline equal emphasis on victims, offenders and community, emphasis on relationships and a forward-looking approach.

Judging from the label by which this position is known, its aim is justice, and it seeks this aim by some kind of restitution or similar re-balancing of some kind of imbalance. This short description may remind us of different kinds of retributivism, as for instance the approaches of Kant and Hegel. In terms of the latter, punish-ment is a necessary negation of a negation.[6] Punishment confirms

5　See footnote 2.
6　See Georg Wilhelm Friedrich Hegel, *Grundlinien der Philosophie des Rechts oder*

and secures the rights of the citizens. Here, we may in other words speak of a retributive justice version of the larger term 'restorative justice'. This approach does not seem to be particularly popular nowadays, despite, for instance, certain adherents of this emphasis on norm-confirmation in German criminal law science (as in the position held, *e.g.*, by Günther Jakobs).[7] The retributive drive in the current, in particular media-driven, development of the criminal justice system seems to have less in common with these sophisticated theoretical positions on criminal justice. Additionally, the approach to the criminal law that today usually goes under the label 'restorative justice' seems to have less in common with this line of thought. Still, it may be useful to bring with us this position, too, in order to understand the currently more popular version of restorative justice.

The currently more popular version of restorative justice, both in theory and in practice, is on its own not quite easy to grasp. It is for instance not easy to explain what the 'restorative' aspect of this approach consists of. Despite the manifest difficulties in grasping the essence of restorative justice, what we can perhaps say, is that, starting out from Nils Christie's famous lecture regarding 'Conflict as Property', the approach to restorative justice that we shall look at in this book is first and foremost asking the basic questions: whose conflict is it in the first place – and what is the proper way for solving the conflict by those who own it?[8] One classic response to these questions within the restorative justice movement is that it is those individuals who are personally involved in the conflict who own the conflict and, hence, it should be solved by them. It is also worth noting that those that are personally involved are not just the offender and the victim of the act. Rather, the restorative justice approach is often connected to a more 'communitarian' view, where the violation of the victim concerns the (local) society itself.

This redistribution of the conflict is in itself a main aim of the restorative justice position, and it often leaves the way of solving it

Naturrecht und Staatswissenschaft im Grundrisse [1821], Frankfurt am Main, 1986, §§ 82–103, in particular § 100.

7   See Günther Jakobs, *Strafrecht - Allgemeiner Teil, Die Grundlagen und die Zurechnungslehre*, 2. Auflage, (Berlin: De Gruyter, 1993).

8   Nils Christie, 'Conflicts as Property', *The British Journal of Criminology*, 17 (1) 1977, pp. 1–15.

to those who are involved in the conflict; it is at least to a certain
degree 'open-ended'. It is also to a large extent open to a range
of different processes for dealing with the conflict. One could in
general say that this openness is the proper way of redistributing
the conflict, giving the owners of it authority both with regard
to procedure and outcome. *Pace* the retributive version sketched
above, it should be emphasised that the focus is not on a norm that
is to be restored. Norms may rightly be one component both in
the views held on what has occurred and in the (re-)constitution
of a community, but only one, and probably not the most important of the several components relevant to this matter – at least
not when speaking of norms in the sense of legal rules. The most
important component is rather the bonds between participants
of the community, bonds created by interaction, care, emotional
ties – and even wrongs. As such, we might perhaps even call it, as
an interpretation of the underlying idea of this approach, justice
as restoration of a community, at minimum; the 'community' of
a victim and an offender. In the following, however, we shall use
the more established term 'restorative justice' when referring to
this approach.

However, this description of restorative justice is certainly
imprecise, but as mentioned, it is not easy to give a short description of this phenomenon. Indeed, it is rather some kind of movement, with several approaches with – at best – some kind of family
resemblance in between them. In the words of Andrew Ashworth,
who with regard to the question of what restorative justice is, states
that '[this] is probably a too large and unspecific question to have a
clear answer. Vessels of widely differing shapes, sizes and modes of
propulsion sail under this particular flag, not least because RJ (as
it tends to be called) is to some extent a practice-led movement'.[9]
For more precise understandings of the phenomenon, we direct
the reader to the literature on the subject. In this book we shall try
to come nearer to a more precise understanding of the potential
of this movement with regard to the criminal justice system. We
will do so by means of discussions looking for exchanges – and
even clashes – between the criminal justice system in its traditional

9   Andrew Ashworth, 'Is Restorative Justice the Way Forward for Criminal
     Justice', *Current Legal Problems*, (2001), p. 347.

shape and ideas and procedures that have their origin or at least familiarity with (branches of) the restorative justice movement.

Before sketching these different discussions that the contributions to this book address, something should be said about why one should pay attention to the ideas of restorative justice with regard to the continuous development of the criminal justice system. After all, the approach of restorative justice challenges in different ways the core assumptions of the traditional model and in particular the idea that the state has the 'monopoly' of administering justice.

1.4 Why look for exchanges?

Why are we investigating this movement of restorative justice? For our part, we see the following reasons in particular for carrying out such an investigation into the phenomenon of restorative justice and its potential for challenging the criminal justice system in its traditional shape.

When working on developing a criminal law theory for Norwegian criminal law, one important means to develop such a theory is to understand the ideas and principles that are already embedded in the criminal law. However, we cannot stop short there. There is also the question of the correctness of these embedded principles: can the criminal justice system as it is traditionally conceived and as it finds its expression in the current criminal justice systems be justified? When developing a criminal law theory, one cannot reject the possibility of this being a critical, or even radical, project. An evaluation of its correctness must in other words also involve a thorough discussion of the more radical alternatives to the established ideas and principles of punishment. The restorative justice movement, at least in its core aspects, does represent a radical alternative to the traditional criminal justice system – not unlike the rehabilitation movement did in the first part of the last century. Such radical alternatives are useful in order to question the existing concept of criminal justice.

The core ideas of the restorative justice approach do in essential aspects represent a different perspective from the established principles of the criminal justice system with regard to dealing with social conflicts. Returning to the traditional model of the criminal justice system it can, for example, be stated that the restorative justice model is in potential conflict with the idea that the response towards a crime is almost exclusively an issue for the state. Furthermore, the restorative justice approach is in conflict with the formalistic or rule-oriented character of the criminal procedure. In addition, the restorative justice approach seems to be in some tension with the basic aims of general deterrence and the strong link between punishment and moral blame, and as the extension of this, the tendency to require a certain level of repression.

It should be added that the restorative justice movement does express certain values that call for attention: inclusion, communication, empathy, compassion, and absence of (physical) force. From a criminal law point of view, it can easily be acknowledged that these values are not the prime quality of the criminal justice system in its traditional shape. The focus on these evidently important values inherent in the restorative justice movement is in other words a good reason for making use of restorative justice as way of challenging and discussing the criminal justice system in its traditional shape.

Even if the exchange with the restorative justice movement does not result in a radical reforming of the criminal justice system in its traditional shape, one should expect that the criminal justice system will still have something to learn from an exchange with restorative justice. Once more the parallel with the exchanges with the rehabilitation movement can be made. There are clear signs of a fruitful inclusion of some particular ideas and approaches of restorative justice into the established criminal justice system, as the contributions to this book illustrate.

A specific Norwegian perspective could be made here. At least apart from some of these changes that will be addressed by the participants in this book, for instance the *Konfliktråd* that has been established, the most notable feature in the Norwegian criminal justice system has perhaps been the strong drive towards improving the place of the victim in the criminal procedure. In this process a central contribution was made by Anne Robberstad, in particular her thesis *Mellom tvekamp og inkvisisjon* ('Between battle and inquisition'). Later on, the White Paper NOU 2006: 10 discussed the place of the victim in the criminal law and made suggestions for improving this position.[10] To a certain extent the improvement of the role of the victim in the criminal procedure seems like a desirable development. The possibility for a fruitful exchange between the criminal procedure and restorative justice should still be further investigated into.

At the same time, however, this development within the Norwegian criminal justice system illustrates a certain problem inherent in such an exchange, with such radically opposing positions in the middle, a problem that gives further motivation for not only looking for exchanges between criminal justice and restorative justice, but also for investigating different kinds of problems originating at deeper levels when seeking such reform. In particular, one cannot disregard the potential problem of the criminal law and the criminal procedure being built upon potentially conflicting ideas and principles, resulting in a manifestly incoherent criminal justice system. As we see it as one of the tasks of legal science to produce coherent conceptions of, for example, the criminal law and criminal procedure, there is good reason to investigate these models in order to reach a more complete conception of both of them, in order to evaluate them and their potential, and to make an informed choice from them. As part of this larger process of designing a coherent theory of the criminal justice system in general, including its different more concrete levels – the criminal procedure in particular – we shall embark in this book on the road towards a more thorough understanding of restorative justice that is capable of taking us further in the understanding of contemporary criminal law and its future.

1.5   An overview of the book

In Chapter 2, David Chelsom Vogt approaches the relationship between restorative and criminal justice, from a philosophical perspective, and explores to what extent these are reconcilable. As Vogt's text makes clear, reconciliation between criminal and restorative justice is hard to achieve at a principled level. The two

---

10   See Anne Robberstad, *Mellom tvekamp og inkvisisjon: straffeprosessens grunnstruktur belyst ved fornærmedes stilling* (Oslo: Universitetsforlaget, 1999) and NOU 2006: 10 *Fornærmede i straffeprosessen – nytt perspektiv og nye rettigheter.*

ideologies are at a basic level founded on quite different concepts of justice – where the criminal justice ideology has its origin in a universal concept of justice, restorative justice for its part seems to depart from a more context-based and intersubjective account of justice. The only possible way of achieving a harmonisation of criminal justice and restorative justice is to accept the presence of conflicting principles within the same system.

Vogt's conclusion concerning the difficulties of reconciling the restorative and the criminal justice ideologies is in a sense supported by the next text, that of Katja Jansen Fredriksen and Eirik Hovden. They address the current absence of a criminal justice system in Yemen comparable to those found in Western legal systems. Here, one finds instead means for conflict resolution that resemble ideas claimed by current restorative justice theorists. Jansen Fredriksen and Hovden give an overview of these means for conflict resolution and make it clear at the same time that this way of solving conflicts is intimately tied to the societal and cultural context of Yemen. In a similar way then, it seems as if one cannot understand the Western criminal justice system without taking into account the societal and cultural context of Western modernity. These different ways of approaching conflicts seem as such closely tied to, respectively, a small-scale society dependent on informal social bonds and integration, and a large-scale society with a high level of differentiation and impersonal relations between the participants in the community. These presuppositions are to a large extent beyond the possibility of the criminal law to create, even if of course it seeks to, and does, contribute to the forming of the cultural and societal context.

However, the conclusion that the criminal and restorative justice ideologies are difficult to reconcile at a principled level, at the same time as their relevance seems to be intimately tied to the societal and cultural context, does not mean that an exchange is impossible either by means of adoption of more concrete mechanisms or by ideological imprints that at concrete points can provide a counterbalancing where certain perspectives have not been taken sufficiently into account. The next three texts all discuss the possibility of integrating restorative justice elements at a more concrete level within the criminal justice system.

Hendrik Kaptein addresses the position of the victim and discusses how this position can be improved. Kaptein questions if it is possible to make changes with regard to the traditionally honoured principle of *in dubio pro reo* in order to secure more convictions as one possible means for protecting the rights of the victim. As Kaptein argues, the possibility of modifying this principle without negative consequences seems limited. As such, it is advisable to look for other possible solutions that could secure the protection of the interest of the victim. Kaptein sees one such mechanism in a state liability for crime and financial compensation.

The lack of taking the victim's point of view into account has not been the only downside of the traditional criminal justice system. On the offender's side, too, there have been some less desirable solutions. This is particularly evident with regard to juvenile offenders, to whom the traditional approach of criminal justice seems to have had less to offer. In a historical perspective, it is no exaggeration to say that the way of dealing with juveniles represents one of the most manifest failures and even injustices of the criminal justice system. At this point, the restorative justice movement may seem to have a lot to offer. Ingun Fornes describes the actual, possible and future impact of restorative justice with regard to dealing with juvenile offenders within the criminal justice system. This text also makes clear the complexity of the criminal justice system that necessarily must lead to a quite nuanced judgement as to what extent and how restorative justice ideas and means could be implemented in the criminal justice system.

This complexity is also a core point in the last and longest contribution to this book. Elizabeth Baumann discusses the possible impact of restorative justice on the level of international criminal justice in the wake of gross violations not only of individuals, but also mass atrocities: what potential is there for making use of restorative justice elements in this process, and can the traditional criminal justice approach be substituted by such means? The experience of South Africa and the use of truth and reconciliation commissions may at a superficial level give a certain romantic picture of the potential of such means. However, a closer look reveals a much more complex picture, and as Baumann's text makes clear, there is at this level, where politics, justice and peace are intimately interwoven, no easy answer to how such conflicts should be dealt with.

2. The aims of restorative justice

Some philosophical remarks on the challenges of integrating restorative justice into the criminal justice system. Reconciling the irreconcilable?

DAVID C. VOGT

2.1 Introduction

'The restorative justice movement originally began as an effort to rethink the needs which crimes create, as well as the roles implicit in crimes', Howard Zehr, one of the pioneers of the movement, writes in his *Little Book of Restorative Justice*.[1] Throughout the last four or five decades, the proponents of restorative justice have questioned the most fundamental aspects of the way we sanction crime: how should we react to crime? What is the aim of our sanctioning system? What are the needs of the parties involved and how can they be met? The answers given have been radically different from the traditional answers of the criminal law. An alternative to the criminal process has been born.

This alternative is, however, not a specific kind of process called restorative justice. Victim–offender mediation, family group conferencing, community circles, sentencing circles – these are just a few of the types of processes that are called restorative.[2] As Lord Justice Auld remarks in his *Review of the Criminal Courts of England and Wales*, restorative justice has been described as 'more of a philosophy than a specific model'.[3]

---

1   Howard Zehr, *The Little Book of Restorative Justice* (Intercourse, PA: Good Books, 2002), p. 13.

2   *E.g.* Shari Tickell and Kate Akester, *Restorative Justice: The Way Ahead* (London: Justice, 2004), p. 21.

3   Lord Justice Auld, *Review of the Criminal Courts of England and Wales* (London:

The philosophy that unites these different models – to the extent that there can be said to be one philosophy of restorative justice: the debate about the definition of restorative justice continues[4] – gives an answer to the question of what the aims of our sanctioning system ought to be. It is the content of these aims that I shall explore in the following. I shall do so by comparing the aims of restorative justice with the aims of the criminal law as they are traditionally conceived, thereby attempting to show that restorative justice is based on a different conception of justice from that of the criminal law, in other words, a different understanding of how individual conflicts ought to be solved, both with regard to *who* should decide the outcome, and *what* a just outcome may be like. I shall also discuss whether restorative justice can be said to fulfil the functional purpose of criminal law in a modern society, especially with regard to general deterrence.

The application of restorative justice processes within the criminal justice system is in continuous growth.[5] Many countries plan to expand the use of restorative justice in the coming years. One example is Norway, where restorative justice is already incorporated into the criminal justice system through the Norwegian Mediation Service (*Konfliktrådet*). A government rapport from 2007 states:

> The Justice Department believes that restorative justice should have a
> central place in the future way of reacting to crime (...) For crimes that
> have been admitted and where there is a known victim, a process of
> dialogue and restoration and reconciliation should always be attempted.
> Such an approach may be viable on all levels and at all times after the
> crime is committed.[6]

Stationery Office Books, 2001), p. 387. The review was commissioned by the Lord Chancellor, the Home Secretary and the Attorney-General in December 1999.

4   *E.g.* Howard Zehr and Barb Toews, *Critical Issues in Restorative Justice* (Monsey, NY: Criminal Justice Press, 2004), pp. 1–60.

5   See, generally, Tickell and Akester, *Restorative Justice*.

6   St.meld. 37 (2007–2008) *Straff som virker* ['Punishment That Works'] – *mindre kriminalitet – tryggere samfunn (Kriminalomsorgsmelding)*, section 12.3.4. In the original Norwegian text the wording is: 'Departementet mener at tilbud om restorative justice bør ha en sentral plass i framtidens måte å reagere på lovbrudd på. (...) Ved tilstått lovbrudd med identifiserbart offer skal det alltid om

In other words: the Justice Department foresees a considerable increase in the use of restorative justice; it desires an even greater integration of restorative justice into the criminal justice system than we have today.[7]

A question then arises: is it possible to integrate restorative justice into the criminal justice system to the extent that the Justice Department plans? Can the two types of processes be reconciled in a way that makes it possible for them to co-exist as two alternative procedures competing for criminal cases? Or do they have such fundamentally different aims that they cannot co-exist without constantly undermining each other? Will for instance the 'case specific' or singular nature of restorative justice processes undermine the rule-of-law principles that constitute the normative basis of the criminal process, such as the principle of legality, the principle of equality before the law and the principle of proportionality between offence and sanction?

A closely related, and more practical, question is *how* it might be possible to organise the integration of restorative justice into the criminal justice system in a way that respects the nature of the two processes, if that is at all possible. For instance, how far can we go in establishing court supervision and control of restorative justice agreements before the autonomy of the mediating parties is jeopardised? And from a criminal justice point of view: how much autonomy is it acceptable to leave to the parties before the process becomes merely a private and not a legal justice process? These and similar questions about the practical integration of restorative justice in the criminal justice system will not, however, be addressed in this paper. The aim here is to clarify some of the philosophical principles that distinguish restorative justice from criminal justice.

The life of the law is not always conducted strictly in accordance with one set of overarching principles. Rules, institutions and

---

mulig legges opp til dialog med gjenoppretting og forsoning som mål. En slik tilnærming kan være aktuelt på alle nivåer og på alle tidspunkter etter at lovbruddet er blitt begått.'

7   The police or prosecutor may today divert criminal cases to the Norwegian Mediation Service when the cases are deemed suitable for mediation (Straffeprosessloven §71a), typically cases of rather minor crime, and not, for instance, serious violent crime.

sanctions that are based on different theoretical viewpoints may be adapted into the legal system in modified versions and as such co-exist quite well. Accordingly, from a traditional pragmatist or functionalist point of view, the co-existence of restorative justice ideas and traditional criminal law ideas in the same criminal justice system may very well be unproblematic. The uncertainty regarding the possibility of reconciling the philosophical foundations of restorative justice with the rule of law principles of the criminal justice system does not necessarily mean that the two processes are irreconcilable in practice. Nevertheless, the practical integration of restorative justice into the criminal justice system would be well served by a philosophical and principled discussion on the nature and the aims of restorative justice and the criminal justice system. It is through such a discussion that we shall become best equipped to judge whether the attempts to integrate restorative justice into the criminal justice system preserve the necessary characteristics of a restorative justice process, or whether the result is an integrated process that ceases to be restorative.

2.2   The general aims of sanctioning crime

On a very general level restorative justice and the criminal justice process share the same aims. They are both ways of sanctioning wrongful behaviour. The purpose of this sanctioning is twofold: on the one hand there is what we might call the societal function of the sanctioning system, where the aim is to deal with wrongful actions in a way that minimises the conflict level in the society as a whole – in other words, to somehow prevent as much wrongdoing in society as possible. On the other hand there is what we might call the individual function of the sanctioning system, where the aim is to deal with each specific conflict in a way that somehow resolves the conflict and restores a sense of justice among the parties. Naturally, these two aspects are not completely independent of each other: individual cases are not solved in a vacuum, but depend on the institutions and norms of the legal system and the established concepts of justice in society. Likewise, the societal function is dependent on individual cases being solved satisfactorily – the legitimacy and efficacy of the legal system rest on the confidence people place in it for solving their conflicts. In addition, individual cases may serve as examples, producing a deterrent effect and thereby influencing the conflict level of society directly.[8]

Though the two processes in question share these very general aims, each process is based on an understanding of the content of these aims and how they should be reached that is sometimes fundamentally different from the other. They do not, in other words, share the same normative basis on some key issues. I shall in the following point out some of these differences both on the societal level and on the individual level.

2.3 The societal function of sanctioning crime

2.3.1 Restorative justice and the community

There is considerable doubt whether restorative justice can fulfil the functional purpose of the criminal law in a complex modern society. Restorative justice is often considered a kind of private conflict resolution that is primarily relevant to the immediate parties of the conflict. In Nils Christie's seminal article *Conflicts as Property*, the criminal process is famously portrayed as 'stealing' the conflict from the involved parties.[9] In contrast, restorative justice is seen as a way of ensuring the parties' ownership of their conflict. The state is often excluded from the process, sometimes attributed only the role of mediator, as in the county-level Norwegian Mediation Service (*Konfliktrådet*). This kind of privatisation of the conflict resolution, awarding the parties greater autonomy in the decision-making, can be seen as being at the heart and soul of restorative justice.[10] It would, however, be wrong to conclude from

---

8   In criminal law science, the aims of the criminal law are most commonly divided between general deterrence and retribution. Both these aims will be treated in the paper. I have, however, chosen to lead the following discussion along the line of the societal and the individual function of the sanctioning system, as these are more general terms that are relevant to both types of process in question.

9   Nils Christie, 'Conflicts as Property', *The British Journal of Criminology*, 17 (1) 1977, pp. 1–15.

10 Howard Zehr views the participation of the primary parties in the justice process as one of the 'three pillars of restorative justice'. The other two pillars are (1) the focus on repairing the harm done to the victims and meeting the needs

this that restorative justice is a private matter and does not include a broader societal perspective. The societal function of the conflict resolution process is important in many restorative justice theories, although society is usually considered on a smaller scale, as the community of the parties.

John Braithwaite is one of many restorative justice theorists who underline the importance of the community in assuring that the agreement reached by the parties is fulfilled. His widely discussed theory of *reintegrative shaming* is a good example of a theory of the purpose of restorative justice that stresses the societal aspect. The restorative justice process, he claims, involves a form of shaming of the offender by the community, and this may have a positive effect when followed by a reintegration of the offender into the community.[11]

R A Duff too stresses the communicative aspect of restorative justice: The characteristic feature of mediation in criminal cases, he claims, is the moral censure that is communicated to the offender for his crime. Mediation in civil cases, on the other hand, does not necessarily involve moral censure or shaming (for instance in a case of two neighbours arguing over water supply). Criminal mediation, like the criminal process, addresses a wrong that has been committed and thus serves the societal purpose of censuring wrongful acts.[12]

Some more radical forms of restorative justice, such as the traditional Native American versions, put an even larger emphasis on the role of the community, not just in the resolution of the conflict, but also in the reason for the emergence of the conflict. In this kind of relationship-oriented form of restorative justice, the offender does not bear the entire responsibility for the offence. The relationships between the offender, the victim and their community must also be taken into account. One could describe it as a form of collective responsibility for not preventing the conflict, as well as for the resolution of the conflict, yet without denying

---

of all parties, and (2) the focus on the offender's obligation toward the victim to repair the harm, *The Little Book of Restorative Justice*, pp. 22–26.

11   John Braithwaite, *Crime, Shame and Reintegration* (Cambridge University Press, 1989).

12   R A Duff, 'Restoration and Retribution', in A. von Hirsch, A. Ashworth & J. Roberts, *Principled Sentencing: Readings on Theory and Policy* (Hart, Oxford: 2009), pp. 178–188.

that the offender has a personal responsibility as well.[13]

Some modern restorative justice theorists, like Howard Zehr, express a similar attitude about the collective responsibility of the community:

> The community bears a responsibility for the welfare of its members and the social conditions and relationships which promote both crime and community peace. The community has responsibilities to support efforts to integrate offenders into the community, to be actively involved in the definitions of offender obligations and to ensure opportunities for offenders to make amends.[14]

2.3.2 General deterrence

The main inadequacy of restorative justice with regard to the societal function of the legal system is the lack of a general deterrence perspective. The outcomes of restorative justice processes can hardly be said to constitute a clear threat of negative sanctions for someone contemplating a crime, mainly because the outcomes are not decided in advance and may vary from relatively extensive restitution schemes to no consequences at all apart from the restorative justice meeting. Hence, it may be claimed that restorative justice does not offer the necessary predictability of sanctions for it to fulfil the deterrent function of the legal system. In addition, the burden of the sanction agreed upon in the restorative justice meeting is often considered to be much lighter than the sanction would have been in a criminal court. Therefore, in the presumed cost–benefit analysis of potential criminals, a threat of restorative justice would weigh less than the threat of punishment, and would presumably lead to more crimes being committed.

However, this idealised rational agent model of general deterrence may be criticised. Empirical research shows that the main deterrent effect comes from the fear of being caught, not from the fear

---

13 For more on the Native American type of restorative justice, see, for example, Rupert Ross, (Toronto: Penguin Canada, 1996), and David C. Vogt, *Det kalkulerende individ: straffesystemets filosofiske forutsetning* (University of Bergen, Master's thesis, 2006, pp. 80–89).

14 Zehr, *The Little Book of Restorative Justice*, p. 66.

of the punishment itself.[15] The greatest fear is of being exposed as the person who committed such an awful act, of being stigmatised as a criminal, of facing the public humiliation of a trial. There is no reason why a restorative justice process cannot be equally frightening, granted the process is public, or at least involves the people the offender cares about.[16] Restorative justice may therefore be able to achieve this main deterrent effect.

But, even though the deterrent effect of fearing exposure is more important than the effect of the threat of punishment, that does not mean that the latter is unimportant, especially facing criminals of the tough sort, who are presumed to be immune to the kind of primary control that restorative justice represents. Some would call it naïve to think that the threat of mediation might deter these habitual criminals. Law professor Johs. Andenæs seems to be of that opinion. He writes in the book *Straffen som problem* ('The Problem of Punishment') that an accountant, a priest, a teacher, a public servant – in other words what we may call 'normal law-abiding citizens' – would rather fear exposure than punishment, when contemplating a crime. But then he goes on to write: 'For a previously punished habitual criminal, or an unemployed youth from a drug-user environment, this would be different'.[17]

Perhaps there is something to this argument: people who already feel alienated from society will not be deterred by the risk of exposure and further alienation. Studies of the criminal group of society show that unmarried men, between 18 and 24 years old, living in cities, with weak ties to family, school, housing and work are over-represented in the criminal statistics. The characteristic trait that unites this group, according to Braithwaite, is weaker than normal social ties to the community.[18]

The conclusion that Andenæs draws – that punishment is necessary because primary control is inefficient for this group – is none the less questionable. It is questionable both from a moral perspec-

---

15 See Jørn Jacobsen, 'Diskusjonen om allmennprevensjonen sin faktiske verknad', *Tidsskrift for strafferett*, 4 (2004), pp. 414–17, for an overview of research on the deterrent effect of punishment.
16 *Cf.* Braithwaite, *Crime, Shame and Reintegration*.
17 Johs. Andenæs, *Straffen som problem* (Halden: Exil, 1994), pp. 53–54.
18 Braithwaite, *Crime, Shame and Reintegration*, pp. 44–48.

tive – he admits that punishment is primarily aimed at some of the least privileged people in society – and logically – he claims that punishment is a necessary deterrent for those people who happen to be the main recipients of punishment. It is a logical fallacy to claim the people who are in fact punished as examples of people for whom the threat of punishment functions as a deterrent – obviously the threat of punishment did not deter these people, since they committed the crimes and were punished. This is not to say that punishment can never deter this group, but merely that it, unlike the law-abiding group of society, cannot be used in an argument for the deterrent effect of punishment.

Perhaps the conclusion should be that neither the fear of exposure, nor the threat of punishment is enough to deter the most diehard criminals, in which case the restorative justice approach of appealing to the conscience of the offender, for instance by confronting him or her with the victim's suffering, might prove to be a more productive approach. Put differently: if weak social ties are acknowledged as a common factor increasing the risk of criminal behaviour, then it would not be unreasonable to think that a sanction that attempts to address this problem might succeed better than a sanction that further excludes the offender from the community.

Either way, it is a plain fact that restorative justice cannot satisfy the aim of deterring presumed cost–benefit calculating and socially alienated criminals, such as members of the mafia, by posing a threat of severely disadvantageous sanctions. This, I suspect, is one of the main reasons why it is considered unrealistic to think that restorative justice can ever replace the criminal process as the main sanctioning process in modern society. Other functional obligations of the legal system, beyond that of general deterrence, further underline this conclusion: the need for an efficient and predictable system where security seems to be an ever more important goal, where the scope of a crime may go way beyond the local and morally more comprehensible crimes of less complex societies, and where the interests that demand protection may be economic, communal or may concern a person on the other side of the globe. The societal function of the legal system in a global world cannot be achieved solely by a mediation system that was conceived under considerably less complex circumstances.

That does not mean that restorative justice has no part to play in a modern society. It is certainly possible to imagine restorative processes alongside the criminal process, even to a larger degree than we see in, for example, Norway today. Perhaps the societal function is sufficiently well maintained by the criminal process, so that even a considerable element of restorative justice in the criminal justice system may still be compatible with it. When it comes to the goal of general deterrence, which is mainly achieved through fear of exposure, there certainly seems to be a large degree of flexibility in the choice of sanction, at least as long as the possibility of punishment remains as a distant threat.[19]

2.3.3 Ensuring the state's monopoly of force

Another societal function of the sanctioning system is maintained by the state's ability to provide a response to wrongful behaviour that prevents the public from taking the sanctioning into own hands. This aim of preventing revenge is perhaps the oldest way of justifying the public penal system. The parties involved, as well as the public at large, must feel that justice is being done if they are to accept that the state has a monopoly on enforcing sanctions. Hence, the criminal justice system must not just accomplish the aim of crime prevention; it must also meet a demand for justice.

Is restorative justice capable of meeting such a demand? The seemingly insatiable appetite for harsher punishment expressed in the media and by most political parties seems to suggest that it may be difficult. It is easy to get the impression that punishing criminals is an essential part of people's sense of justice: no punishment, no justice.

19 The question of whether restorative justice can take part in a criminal justice
    system without weakening its deterrent function naturally invokes a more
    fundamental question regarding the extent to which general deterrence should
    influence the design of the criminal justice system in general. Some, like
    Nils Jareborg in *Straffrättsideologiska fragment* (Uppsala: Iustus Förlag, 1992),
    pp. 136–48, argue that general deterrence is a relevant concern only with regard
    to criminalisation: and its function in terms of crime prevention, and deny
    its role in sentencing and execution of the sanction. From such a perspective,
    restorative justice elements in the process and sentencing would presumably be
    regarded as unproblematic under such a theory, as long as the criminalisation
    and threat of punishment is upheld. This is not to suggest that Jareborg and
    others may not find restorative justice problematic for other reasons than general deterrence.

However, as research has shown, the matter is more complicated. The large survey performed by Flemming Balvig in 2006,
Danskernes syn på straf ('The Danish View on Punishment')[20]
suggests that people's view on the justice of punishment greatly
depends on the way the question is asked. When asked a general
question of their view of punishment, a great majority claimed
to be in favour of harsher sentences. But when asked what they
considered to be right in a specific case, they were a lot less punitive, and generally less so than the Danish courts. And after being
shown a video of a simulated trial, most became even milder in
their judgements.[21]

How should we interpret these results? Either people's opinions
are generally not well informed and they therefore change their
opinion when more information is given (on a specific case) – this
suggests that people are in reality less punitive than one might get
the impression of from simple surveys and TV talk shows – or it
means that the very concept of justice is such that it evades a clear
definition that can yield universal answers to what is just. A third
possibility is that both of these interpretations may be right.

2.4 Resolving individual cases

We are now already deep into the question of what I have called
the individual function of the sanctioning system: dealing with
each case in a way that resolves the conflict and restores a sense of
justice. I shall now look more closely at how the two processes in
question attempt to fulfil this function and then return to the issue
of how we should interpret Balvig's survey and the possibility for
restorative justice to satisfy our demand for justice.

Even passionate utilitarians will concede that the criminal pro-

---

20 Flemming Balvig, *Danskernes syn på straf* (Copenhagen: Advokatsamfundet, 2006).
21 In 2009, Flemming Balvig, Helgi Gunnlaugsson, Kristina Jerre, Leif Petter
    Olaussen and Henrik Tham conducted a follow-up survey in all the Nordic
    countries that has largely corroborated the findings of Balvig's 2006 study (the
    Finnish results have not yet been analysed), see Balvig, Gunnlaugsson, Jerre,
    Olaussen and Tham, 'Attitudes towards Punishment in the Nordic Countries',
    Nordisk Tidsskrift for Kriminalvidenskap, 97 (3) (2010). Similar results were
    also found by Thomas Mathiesen, *Tiltak mot ungdomskriminalitet* (Oslo:
    Universitetsforlaget, 1965).

cess must aim at creating a just solution to each case. It might not be the primary aim – general deterrence or treatment of offenders might be considered more important – but as Johs. Andenæs[22] and John Rawls,[23] among others, have stressed: punishment must always be deserved by the offender. It would be wrong to consider only the utility of punishing somebody; it would inevitably lead to the acceptance of punishing innocent people or bestowing draconian sentences when the consequences are for the greater good. Punishment must be just, which means that the offender, to use the term of Immanuel Kant, must be 'strafbar' ('punishable').

The way Kant explains it, a person makes himself 'strafbar' by committing a crime and thereby accepting that others have the right to treat him the same way as he treated others. In Kantian terms, all humans have a rational part, what he calls 'homo noumenon', and it is this pure reason in us that 'draw(s) up a penal law against myself as a criminal'.[24] It is, in other words, the universality of reason that makes it rational and right to treat the offender according to the 'rules' that his rational part drew up. Kant goes further and claims that this not only gives us the right to punish criminals, but that we have a duty to do so. However, we do not have to follow Kant in this controversial last part of his argument, if we, like Andenæs and Rawls, set forth other reasons why we should carry out the punishment of somebody. The offender's 'Strafbarkeit' – his deserving of punishment – becomes the minimum criterion that gives us the right to punish him, while crime prevention and other greater goods offer the reasons for actually going through with it. In either case, whether one accepts utilitarian reasons for punishment, or if one, like Kant, accepts only the moral imperative of retribution, punishment must be considered to realise the function of creating justice.

In the rule of law-, or *Rechtsstaat*-tradition[25], certain criteria must be met for punishment to be just. The debate about these criteria is extensive, and it would take us too far to account for the different

---

22 *Op. cit.*

23 John Rawls, 'Two Concepts of Rules', *The Philosophical Review*, 64 (1955).

24 Immanuel Kant, *The Metaphysics of Morals* [1797] (Cambridge University Press, 1996), p. 108.

25 See footnote 2, Chapter 1.

positions here.[26] There is, however, broad agreement on three main criteria for just punishment. Firstly, the rules under which one is punished must be known in advance; there must be legal certainty so as to make it possible to make rational choices to uphold the law and avoid punishment. Secondly, there must be equality before the law; similar acts deserve similar reactions, regardless of who committed them. And thirdly, there must be proportionality; the punishment must be balanced with the seriousness of the crime. Within the scale of punishment, more serious crimes should be punished more harshly than less serious crimes. If one or more of these criteria are not met – if one is either convicted without having been given a fair chance to avoid it by being made aware of the criteria for conviction in advance, if the punishment is unfair in the sense that there are no relevant reasons for the unequal treatment, or if the punishment does not stand in a reasonable relation to the offence committed – we would consider the sanction unjust and not in accordance with the rule of law.

How then, does restorative justice relate to these three criteria?

With regard to (1) legal certainty, it is clear that restorative justice does not entirely achieve it. The result of the meeting between the parties is not predetermined in a set of rules, so it is nearly impossible to know the sanction in advance. Neither are the criteria for initiating a restorative justice process certain. A restorative justice meeting can in theory be initiated even when it is unclear whether a crime has actually been committed, whether one of the parties is criminally liable, if they both are, etc. However, when restorative justice is applied in a criminal context, there is usually more certainty. The process is initiated at the request of the police or prosecutor (and in some countries by a judge). It must be clear that the law has been transgressed and that the offender has taken responsibility for the act (though not necessarily legal responsibility) and agrees to be part of the restorative justice meeting.

With regard to (2) equality, restorative justice agreements vary to a large degree and acts that would be considered similar in the criminal process might result in completely different sanctions

---

26 For a discussion of the rule of law principles forming the basis of the criminal law, see for instance Jørn Jacobsen, *Fragment til forståing av den rettsstatlege strafferetten* (Bergen: Fagbokforlaget, 2009).

in a restorative justice process, depending, for instance, on the victim's willingness to forgive. Restorative justice is therefore not in accordance with the principle of equality. As a note to this, we could add that restorative justice is in this sense similar to the civil part of the legal system – actions that one person might get sued for are left unsanctioned in other instances, because the possible plaintiff for some reason does not want a lawsuit. We do not hear many complaints about the unfairness of that system, something that suggests that the incomparability of restorative justice sanctions may not be as problematic if considered outside of a criminal law context.

With regard to (3) proportionality, restorative justice does not include any rules determining the proportionality of the offence and the sanction. The criticism of restorative justice is usually that the sanctions are too mild – the offenders do not get what they deserve. It is true that the sanctions agreed upon – for example making some sort of financial restitution – are from an outsider's perspective often considerably less painful for the offender than the result would have been after a criminal process. The focus is primarily on remedying the harm done to the victim, and it is therefore usually less punitive toward the offender. However, one should not underestimate the emotional toll it takes on the offender having to face the victim and their family and hearing their suffering. Many offenders would probably prefer the seclusion of a prison cell to the confrontation of a restorative justice meeting. The restorative justice process itself, and not just the result of the meeting, should therefore be viewed as an important part of the sanction. None the less, although the differences in the burden of the sanctions between the two types of processes might be slightly smaller than assumed, restorative justice cannot be said to fulfil the criterion of proportionality.[27]

27 Restorative justice sanctions are problematic regardless of whether the criterion of proportionality is viewed as absolute or relative. Kant (*The Metaphysics of Morals*, pp. 105–06), for instance, operates with an absolute criterion of proportionality, where each sanction must be balanced against the specific crime. Jareborg (*Straffrättsideologiska*, p. 148) and other modern criminal law theorists see proportionality as relative within the scale of punishment, meaning that more blameworthy crimes ought to be punished more severely than less blameworthy crimes, and equally blameworthy acts should be punished equally. The principle of proportionality does not, according to this view, determine

The conclusion is that restorative justice does not live up to the standard of just sanctioning expressed through these three criteria, legal certainty, equality and proportionality. Restorative justice is in other words in conflict with principles that are central to a traditional understanding of a criminal justice system based on the rule of law, or the democratic *Rechtsstaat*. This may be one of the main reasons why restorative justice processes, in all the countries in which they are applied, have usually been limited to less serious offences.[28] The conflict between the different conceptions of just sanctioning would become all too evident if, let us say, a murderer would come to a financial agreement with the victim's family, and the fulfilment of the agreement were the only sanction he would suffer. The discrepancy between the solutions of the retributive and the restorative forms of justice becomes larger in more serious cases.

2.5 The underlying concepts of justice

Although the two types of processes share the aim of creating justice in individual cases, the content of the aim, as we have seen, is not the same. The concepts of justice that the processes seek to fulfil differ from each other both substantially – with regard to *what* is seen as just, and formally – with regard to *how* justice is determined.

The concept of justice that the criminal process aims at fulfilling is *objective*. It is objective in the sense that it can be expressed in the form of principles such as 'crime ought to be punished' and 'punishment should be proportional to the crime'. These principles are expressed in advance, and the individual cases should deduce their solutions from them so that they exemplify these principles. The concept of justice is thus also *universal*, applicable to all cases unless there are significant reasons for making an exception. The criteria

---

the level of repression itself. Even such a criterion of relative proportionality is unattainable for restorative justice, as there is no way of determining that more blameworthy crimes receive more severe sanctions, nor that equally blameworthy crimes are sanctioned correspondingly.

28   There are some examples of restorative justice processes being applied in such serious cases as murder, child abuse and robbery, but then as an addition to, and not a replacement of the criminal process. See Tickell and Akester, *Restorative Justice*, p. 60.

of legal certainty, equality and proportionality all contribute to realising this concept of justice.

The concept of justice that the restorative justice process aims at fulfilling is, on the contrary, not universal. All conflicts are attempted to be resolved in their own, unique way, considering only factors that are directly relevant to the specific case. One does not try to solve a case similarly to other cases that resemble it. What is just in one case may be unjust in another. This is a *singular*, and not a universal concept of justice.

Naturally, the criminal process usually also leaves some room for considerations of factors that are unique to a case. The offender's life situation, for instance, may be given attention when deliberating on the equity of the sanction. Nevertheless, the criminal process takes as its starting point the transgression of a certain prohibition. Otherwise dissimilar events are thus necessarily framed within the context of the crime in question. A certain likeness is abstracted from the cases in order to subsume them under the prohibition, and a certain set of justice criteria are assigned to them, such as the upper and lower limits of punishment for the type of crime. Restorative justice, on the other hand, is not committed to framing the conflict within the context of a certain type of crime, and thus avoids having to relate the justice of the case to the general criteria of justice pertaining to that type of crime.[29]

Restorative justice also does not have an objective concept of justice. The just solution is not based on principles that are established in advance (at least not explicitly). Instead the just solution is simply that which is considered just by the involved parties. I suggest we call this an *inter-subjective* concept of justice, as opposed to an objective one. If the parties come to an agreement that they consider to be just, then it does not matter whether it is in accordance with the principle of proportionality or other such principles or not – justice is simply what the parties experience as justice in the particular case.

29   The extent to which restorative justice processes, when applied in a criminal justice system, should be framed within the categories of the criminal law is a matter of debate. Some theorists, like R A Duff, propose that criminal mediation ought to be conducted 'under the aegis of the criminal law' (*Op. cit.*, p. 183), including defining the type of crime in question. Others, like Nils Christie, propose a strict separation between the two types of process, leaving the definition of the act in question up to the parties.

In this experience of justice, the emotions of the parties are an important component; an agreement is just when it feels right for the parties. If the agreement enables the parties to move on, if they leave with a feeling of justice having been done, if the process has helped them to deal with their trauma and concerns for the future – then the objective rationality of the content of the agreement becomes subordinate.

Moral philosophy has traditionally concentrated on clarifying moral concepts, such as the concept of justice. This is the Socratic legacy of Western philosophy: philosophy's main task is to clarify concepts, and this will in turn lead us to act in the right way. As a result, the view of morals in Western philosophy has mainly been that they are a purely cognitive faculty – Kant being the epitome of this position, Aristotle being an important exception. Less emphasis has been laid on empathy, on moral impulse and intuition, on not just knowing intellectually what the right thing to do is, but feeling it and reacting on a moral emotion.

The moral philosophy of Emmanuel Lévinas is an expression of this latter position.[30] For him, morality is something that occurs in the meeting between two people, a meeting of I and the Other. When I meet 'the face of the Other' an infinite responsibility for this unique Other arises in me. It is not a reciprocal responsibility, like in a contract. Morality is not about treating everybody the same. On the contrary, Lévinas' understanding of morality is about treating everybody as other, as unique. It is about acting on the moral experience of the concrete situation, not about reasoning about concepts and principles from which moral action is deduced.

This understanding of morality may better explain the way in which the experience of justice is conceived in restorative justice than the more cognitive and deductive moral reasoning that underlies the concept of justice that the criminal process aims at reaching. More emphasis is laid on the parties' emotions, of restoring their sense of self-respect and feeling of safety, on establishing a feeling of closure and dealing with their emotional pain. Much attention is therefore devoted to ensuring that the process itself is conducted in a way that is conducive to these experiences. If the parties really

---

30   Emmanuel Lévinas, *Totality and Infinity* (Pittsburgh: Duquesne University Press, 1969).

are to feel that justice has been done, it is imperative that their autonomy is respected in the decision-making. Legal representation and jargon are avoided, less attention is devoted to fact-finding and establishing guilt, the rhetoric aims less at convincing a third party that one party is right and the other party is wrong, and more at finding a common future ground and repairing the relationship between the parties.[31] The restorative justice meeting itself must be viewed as part of the experience of justice-being-done, and not just as a necessary step towards a just result.

These differences should not, however, be exaggerated. Restorative justice is not all about 'listening to your inner feelings' without any logical reasoning, and likewise, the criminal process is not a completely rational enterprise, where feelings are excluded entirely. In fact, this strict separation of feeling and reasoning is itself somewhat philosophically outdated.[32] There is usually an element of the cognitive in the emotional, and the emotional in the cognitive.

The way I interpret Flemming Balvig's survey, it supports the conclusion that these two elements are present to a varying degree in our deliberations on justice. On the most general level, our search for justice is mostly cognitive. We reason from principles such as that of proportionality. As we delve deeper into the concrete moral situation of punishing an offender, our moral intuition becomes more important. Perhaps it is a sense of empathy with the offender that makes the people in Balvig's study less punitive as they get closer to the offender. In any case, the survey has shown that our sense of justice is complex and often incoherent – we display attitudes that contradict each other, depending on the context in which we are asked.

Perhaps then, it would be wise to conclude that although the justice of restorative justice is different from the justice of the criminal justice system, and there are considerable challenges in incorporating the former into the latter, this need not be viewed primarily as a problem. Restorative justice could be welcomed as a supplement to the objective and universal criminal justice, because the complexity of our sense of justice cannot be exhausted by one

31   For a treatment of this 'rhetoric of reconciliation', see Trygve T. Svensson and David C. Vogt, 'Konfliktløsningens retorikk,' *Rhetorica Scandinavica*, 52 (2010).
32   See for instance Antonio Damasio, *Descartes' Error* (London: Vintage Books, 1994).

such concept alone. If we acknowledge that our sense of justice is incoherent – if we acknowledge the impossibility of capturing all that we consider to be just within one universal concept – then the task of creating a completely coherent system of norms may appear less crucial. The prospect of different processes undermining each other within the system may seem less precarious.

As mentioned at the beginning, the life of the law is seldom conducted strictly in accordance with one set of overarching principles. Perhaps we ought to see this as a strength and not a weakness of a justice system that ought to reflect the citizens' sense of justice. It might be a good thing if our focus shifted slightly in favour of putting the solution of the individual conflict first – including applying the best suited form of process – even if it means accepting some differences in how similar cases are treated. Justice, after all, is not just about equal treatment, but about addressing the issues of the specific case, seeking, in the best possible way, to restore a sense of peace for the people involved.

References

Andenæs, J., *Straffen som problem* (Halden: Exil, 1994).

Auld, Lord Justice, *Review of the Criminal Courts of England and Wales* (London: Stationery Office Books, 2001).

Balvig, F., *Danskernes syn på straf* (Copenhagen: Advokatsamfundet, 2006).

Balvig, F., Gunnlaugsson, H., Jerre, K., Olaussen, L.P., and Tham, H., 'Attitudes towards Punishment in the Nordic Countries', *Nordisk Tidsskrift for Kriminalvidenskap*, 97 (3) (2010).

Braithwaite, J., *Crime, Shame and Reintegration* (Cambridge University Press, 1989).

Christie, N., 'Conflicts as Property', *The British Journal of Criminology*, 17 (1) (1977).

Damasio, A., *Descartes' Error* (London: Vintage Books, 1994).

Jacobsen, J., 'Diskusjonen om allmennprevensjonen sin faktiske verknad', *Tidsskrift for strafferett*, 4 (2004), pp. 394–438.

Fragment til forståing av den rettsstatlege strafferetten (Bergen: Fagbokforlaget, 2009).

Jareborg, N., *Straffrättsideologiska fragment* (Uppsala: Iustus Förlag, 1992).

Kant, I., *The Metaphysics of Morals* [1797] (Cambridge University Press, 1996).

Lévinas, E., *Totality and Infinity* (Pittsburgh: Duquesne University Press, 1969).

Mathiesen, T., *Tiltak mot ungdomskriminalitet* (Oslo: Universitetsforlaget, 1965).

Rawls, J., 'Two Concepts of Rules', *The Philosophical Review*, 64 (1955).

Ross, R., *Returning to the Teachings* (Toronto: Penguin Canada, 1996).

Svensson, T.T., and Vogt, D.C., 'Konfliktløsningens retorikk,' *Rhetorica Scandinavica*, 52 (2010).

Tickell, S., and Akester, K., *Restorative Justice: The Way Ahead* (London: Justice, 2004).

Vogt, D.C., *Det kalkulerende individ: straffesystemets filosofiske forutsetning* (University of Bergen, Master's thesis, 2006).

Zehr, H., *The Little Book of Restorative Justice* (Intercourse, PA: Good Books, 2002).

Zehr, H., and Toews, B., *Critical Issues in Restorative Justice* (Monsey, NY: Criminal Justice Press, 2004).

3. Restorative justice in Islamic criminal law?

KATJA JANSEN FREDRIKSEN & EIRIK HOVDEN[1]

3.1 Introduction

Restorative justice is a movement that has gained in popularity in European and Western countries in recent years as a way of giving victims and their families a larger role in criminal procedures.[2] In brief, restorative justice refers to a process (or different kinds of processes) whereby the parties with a stake in a specific offence collectively resolve how to deal with the aftermath of the offence and its implications for the future.[3] In recent discussions on criminal law in Europe the emergence of restorative justice has been raised as a supplementary element to the traditional way of thinking about the criminal process.[4] To a significant extent Western criminal law is traditionally centred on 'retributive justifications'

---

1   The authors would especially like to thank post doc. Jørn RT Jacobsen and post doc. Linda Gröning for introducing us to the movement of 'restorative justice' and commenting on this chapter and Professor Knut S. Vikør and Professor Jørn Øyrehagen Sunde for commenting on an earlier version of this chapter. The authors of course alone bear the responsibility for the content of this chapter. Parts of this chapter have been published in Katja Jansen Fredriksen and Eirik Hovden, 'Jemenittisk strafferett: en intrikat blanding av nasjonal statslov-givning, islamsk rett og strafferett', *Tidsskrift for Strafferett*, 2 (2010), pp. 154–68.

2   In recent years victims and their relatives have asked for more attention for the victim in what Nils Christie called a 'Victim-Orientated Court'. See Christie, 'Conflicts as Property', in Andrew von Hirsch and Andrew Ashworth, *Principled Sentencing: Readings on Theory and Policy*, 2nd edition (Oxford: Hart Publishing, 1998), p. 315.

3   See T.F. Marshall, *Restorative Justice: an Overview* (London: [British] Home Office, Research and Statistics Directorate, 1999), p. 5.

4   See, for instance, von Hirsch and Ashworth, *Principled Sentencing*, pp. 300–61.

of punishment and ideas that punishment has a general deterrent effect.[5] Theories of restorative justice instead typically underline aspects of reconciliation and the restoration of the relationship between the perpetrator and the victim.[6]

At the same time as elements of reconciliation and restoration are to some extent in tension with the Western paradigm of criminal law, they seem – interestingly enough – to be more common in Islamic criminal law.[7] In fact, one of the main features and characteristics of Islamic law is its emphasis on mediation and arbitration. Islamic criminal law as practised in states like Yemen contains strong elements of private arbitration and reconciliation compared with criminal law in most Western societies. On this background, this chapter deals with the subject of restorative justice in Islamic criminal law. More specifically, it will, on the basis of comparative analysis, argue that there are elements in Islamic criminal law as practised in Muslim states that in essential aspects resemble Western ideas on restorative justice. The article will also draw some tentative conclusions on the differences between the basis and functions of restorative justice in Western and respectively Islamic criminal law, and the impact of culture in this respect. Yemen will be used as an example and this chapter will focus on criminal law practices and conflict resolution in the fields of murder and bodily harm. It appears that the Yemeni practice resembles central aspects of the concept of restorative justice and that this resemblance is strong enough to produce fundamental theoretical questions of the potential and limitations of restorative justice.

5   See, for instance, Andenæs, *Allminnelig strafferett,* pp. 67ff., and Jørn RT Jacobsen, 'Diskusjonen om allmennprevensjonen sin faktiske verknad', *Tidsskrift for strafferett,* (2004), pp. 394–438 for an overview of Andenæs' research on the actual effectiveness of the generally deterrent effect and to what extent new research supports Andenæs 'conclusions.

6   See Anne Robberstad, *Mellom tvekamp og inkvisisjon: straffeprosessens grunnstruktur belyst ved fornærmedes stilling* (Oslo: Universitetsforlaget, 1999), NOU 2006: 10 *Fornærmede i straffeprosessen – nytt perspektiv og nye rettigheter* and the Norwegian White Paper (NOU 2002: 4) on this topic.

7   The term 'Islamic criminal law' is problematic in certain academic perspectives, which cannot be pursued within the scope of this article here.

3.2 Notes on the use of deep-level comparative law

Since this chapter makes use of comparative analysis, it seems adequate to begin with some notes on this matter. The authors outline deep-level comparative law to compare different legal cultures.[8] Despite the difference between Islamic criminal law and criminal law in Western societies, here we shall compare what function reconciliation has in Yemeni criminal law as a way of restoring justice and how this function either diverges or coincides with similar ideas concerning restorative justice in Western, and particularly Norwegian, criminal law. In this chapter we shall therefore use deep-level comparative law as a method to compare not only foreign rules, legal practice and the legal facts or functions of legal concepts, but also the factors that determine the deeper layers of the legal cultures in which the legal concept functions and that determine its practice and further development.

By using Yemeni criminal law as an example the authors will argue that the basis and functions of restorative justice cannot be properly understood without also understanding the local historical, political, social and legal contexts in which the actors are situated. In Muslim countries, processes with elements of restorative justice seem to be situated in local structures, practices and symbols that the state can never fully control. This makes the basis and functions of such restorative processes different in Islamic criminal law from those in Western legal orders. Instead of the state delegating power to the victim or the victim's family in order to restore justice, elements of restorative justice in Islamic criminal law are rather the result of the lack of power by the state. Still, there are functions that both legal systems have in common.

3.3 The case of Yemen: Societal structures

Yemen is one of the poorest countries in the world and most of its inhabitants are sedentary farmers organised in tribes. The strong tribal culture combined with the mountain landscape has made

---

8 See, for instance, Mark Van Hoecke, 'Deep Level Comparative Law', in Mark Van Hoecke, (ed.), *Epistemology and Methodology of Comparative Law* (Oxford: Hart Publishing, 2004), pp. 165–95.

it difficult for a central government to control the country. It has therefore always been necessary for the Yemeni state to play along with the tribes. Yemen has traditionally been an agricultural society, but in recent years the population has increased dramatically and political instability has led to high unemployment rates and lack of sustainable economic and political development. During the last two decades, income from oil exports has been important to maintain the governmental sector; however, in the last few years oil revenues have been diminishing and oil profits have mainly been divided among a smaller circle of persons closely connected to the President.[9] In 1996 Yemen agreed to give up its claim to the three economically important Saudi governorates, 'Asir, Najran and Jizan in order to get a better and more stable relationship with its neighbour Saudi Arabia.[10] Despite this agreement the relationship with Saudi Arabia remains complicated and Saudi Arabia has little interest in seeing Yemen develop into a strong state. Tribal leaders in Yemen receive monthly salaries from Saudi Arabia in return for their political loyalty and support. In addition, individual actors in Saudi Arabia economically support the expansion of the fundamentalist Wahhabism in Yemen.[11]

During the last fifty years, Yemen has gradually developed from a religiously legitimised *Imamate*,[12] in the north, to a Republic, which in 1990 merged with the socialistic and previously British colonial South Yemen. In the next section, we shall further investigate how this political development affected the legal system in Yemen.

---

9   See, for instance, April Longley Alley, 'The Rules of the Game: Unpacking Patronage Politics in Yemen', *The Middle East Journal*, Vol. 64, No. 3, (25), (Summer 2010), pp. 385–409.

10 The *Ta'if* agreement from 1934 handed these northern governorates *de facto* over to Saudi Arabia on the provision that the agreement would be renegotiated every twenty years. This led to strained relationships between the neighbouring countries. See Katja Jansen, *Grensproblematiek tussen Saoedi-Arabie en Jemen: 'Asir, Najran en Jizan; een case study ('Border disputes between Saudi Arabia and Yemen: 'Asir, Najran and Jizan: a case study')*, (University of Leiden Press, 1996).

11 Wahhabism is a conservative form of Islam, which is practised mainly in Saudi Arabia.

12 The term 'Imam' here does not refer to the common use of the term ('imam'), who is leading the prayer, but rather to the political, religious and judiciary leader of the *Zaydi* state.

3.4 Historical development of Yemen's legal system and state administration

3.4.1 Prior to modernisation

Northern Yemen is divided between Sunni and Zaydi Muslims. The Zaydi school of law is a Shi'a variant, independent of that in Iran and Iraq today. Southern Yemen and the lowlands in Northern Yemen are Shafi'i Sunnis. This religious diversity has also long influenced the way the state structure has been organised. Until 1962, (north) Yemen was a religiously legitimated Imamate where the religious and legal leader was also the head of the state administration and the judicial system. Until 1967 the territory later known as South Yemen was a British protectorate. At that time public prosecution was poorly developed and was used only in the most important religious matters. This implied that it was the party's own responsibility to bring a case before the court. This also applied to murder cases. The court system was mostly used for different types of contractual and property transactional law, including marriage and inheritance disputes.[13]

3.4.2 Attempts to modernise the legal system

In 1962, the *Imamate* was overthrown with the support of Egypt, and the Yemeni Arab Republic was founded shortly after. Many expected that modernity finally would reach this remote and isolated part of the Arabian Peninsula. However, after a long civil war that ended around 1970 the newly established republic reverted to rather traditional ideas and practices. The new balance of power was affected by the fact that socialistic Egypt had lost much of its important political position in the Arab world and that the conservative Wahhabi Saudi Arabia had become stronger. At the same time, Southern Yemen became communist after having thrown the British out in 1967. The border between the two countries therefore represented an important border in the Cold War. The two states were merged in 1990, but after a short civil war in 1994, the conservative forces of the North defeated the leftist intellectuals

---

13   These areas of the law are called *mu'amalat*, 'transactions'.

of the South. This process led to a period where the South faced
a reversion from a system built on British and socialistic ideals
towards a system where traditional Islamic values were given a
more prominent place. This tension between the more liberal South
and the traditional North is still very much felt in current Yemeni
politics and has also affected the further development of Yemeni
law.[14] Modernity, including a Western legal order, was therefore
never fully introduced, neither as an idea nor in practice.[15] Still,
Yemen has ratified several international human rights conventions
and even if Article 3 of the Yemeni Constitution states that '[the]
Islamic Shari'a is the source for all legislation',[16] the Yemeni State
has not made any reservations in relation to the *Shari'a* with regard to
its human rights obligations, as many other Muslim states have done.

3.5   The role of the state in Yemen's legal order

3.5.1 *A hybrid legal system*

During the last thirty years the State of Yemen has been led by
President Salih and has a democratically elected Parliament with its
seat in the capital Sana'a. The main positions among politicians and
bureaucrats are held by tribe leaders, the army and the economic elite.
The old aristocratic families from the *Imam*-administration have, to a

---

14   See, for instance, Anna Würth, 'Stalled Reform: Family Law in Post-
     Unification Yemen', *Islamic Law and Society*, 12 (2003), pp. 12–33.

15   Nisrine Abiad, *Sharia, Muslim States and International Human Rights Treaty
     Obligations: A Comparative Study* (London: British Institute of International and
     Comparative Law (BIICL), 2008), p. 48.

16   This provision is relatively ambiguous stating that the 'Islamic *Shari'a* is the
     source (*al-masdar*) of all legislation'. This may indicate that the *Shari'a* is the
     exclusive source of legislation, but may also indicate that the *Shari'a* represents
     one of many legal sources in Yemen. Taking a closer look at historical develop-
     ments in Yemen, we notice that the Yemeni Constitution has been amended
     several times on this point. From 1970 to 1991 the Yemeni Constitution
     defined *Shari'a* as 'the source (*al-masdar*) to legislation'. From 1991 to 1994 the
     word 'main' was added (*al-masdar al-ra'isi*), which made the *Shari'a* 'the main
     source of all legislation' in Yemen. In 1994 the term was again removed from
     the Constitution, which implies that the wording is once more the same as in
     1970. See Anna Würth, *As-Sari'a fi Bab al-Yaman, Recht, Richter und Rechtpraxis
     an der familienrechtlichen Kammer des Gerichts Süd-Sanaa, (Republik Jemen) 1983-
     1995* (Berlin: Duncker and Humblot, 2000), p. 52, footnote 62.

large extent, managed to maintain their positions in Yemeni society, mainly within the legal system, legal education and legal science.

Although Yemen is a state, the executive power does not have a monopoly on sentencing in society as practiced in Western legal orders. The division between the judicial and executive power is in practice little developed and newly implemented. It is more of a hybrid legal system that has been developed by different actors during many centuries into a system that is founded upon the maintenance of a certain balance of power between different groups. The state therefore does not perceive it to be its prime function to keep order and structure and to protect the individual against the state and other individuals, as in a *Rechtsstaat*.[17]

3.5.2 *The legislative power*

Islamic law is an important part of contemporary Yemeni state legislation, the latter also being influenced by Egyptian law, which in turn is influenced by French law.[18] One of the formal tasks of the Yemeni Parliament[19] is to ratify new laws and amendments, but only after these in advance have been found to be conform with Islamic principles by a separate *Shari'a*-committee.[20] Article 2 of the Yemeni Constitution states that 'Islam is the Religion of State in Yemen'. As mentioned earlier, Article 3 of the Constitution requires that all legislation is in convergence with the Shari'a.[21] In 1987 Yemen ratified both the International Covenant on Civil and Political Rights (ICCPR) and the International Covenant on Economic, Social and Cultural Rights (ICESCR) which set certain standards with regard to the principle of fair trial and other procedural rights.[22]

---

17 See footnote 2, Chapter 1.
18 An example of this is the division of traditional Islamic legal rule collections into 'laws' with Western names such as, for instance, the Yemeni Civil Code, *al-Qanun al-Madani* and the Personal Status Law (*Qanun al-ahwal al-shakhsiyya*).
19 The Parliament is a democratic elected council.
20 This *Shari'a* council consists of legal experts with training in Islamic jurisprudence (*fiqh*), whose main task it is to reassure that new law proposals are in compliance with traditional, classical Islamic law.
21 See Abdullahi A. An-Na'im, (ed.), *Islamic Family Law in a Changing World: A Global Resource Book* (London: Zed Books Ltd, 2002), p. 145.
22 *Ibid.*, p. 147. Yemen has made reservations in both Convenants against the recognition of the State of Israel.

3.5.3 Courts and private arbitrators

National courts are situated throughout the country, but the population has generally little confidence in the formal legal system.
In addition, the legal system is little used due to corruption, high
litigation costs and long court proceedings. Civil cases can be particularly time-consuming and used in a manner to delay the case
as much as possible. Therefore alternative systems of law are often
used instead, such as private arbitrators, with or without a state
licence as governed by the Yemeni Arbitration Law (in Arabic:
qanun al-tahkim).[23] These arbitrators (*muhakkam*, pl. *muhakkamun*)
are respectable men with personal integrity and a high social status, who are perceived to be neutral by both parties in the dispute
at stake. Arbitrators generally earn considerable social status and
trust within the Yemeni population and often have considerable
years of practice in dispute arbitration. The solutions that they
offer are often less time-consuming, less expensive and focus more
on reconciliation between the parties than cases decided by the
state. This has led to the fact that these informal legal systems
are often preferred to the formal legal system administered by the
Yemeni State. Over time a hybrid system of customary law has
developed, that in turn has been incorporated into the other existing legal systems of Islamic jurisprudence (*fiqh*) and Yemeni state
law.

3.5.4 Legal doctrine and case law

In Yemeni law there is a much stronger distinction between official
state legislation, legal doctrine and case law than, for instance, in
Norwegian law. Yemeni judges have to recognise not only official
state law, but also parts of Islamic jurisprudence, customary law
and tribal law.[24] When parties start legal procedures in the official

---

23 For comments about the arbitration law, see Laila al-Zwaini, 'Mediating
between Custom and Code: Dar al-Salam, an NGO for Tribal Arbitration in
Sanaa', *Monde Arabe*, 1 (2005).

24 The scope of this chapter will not allow us to conceptualise this legal plurality
in a theoretical framework. However, in practice, the actors can rarely choose
freely between different systems of law. See also Baudouin Dupret, 'Legal
Pluralism, Normative Plurality, and the Arab World,' in Baudouin Dupret,
Merits Berger and Laila al-Zwaini, (eds.), *Legal Pluralism in the Arab World* (The
Hague, London, Boston: Kluwer Law International, 1999); Baudouin Dupret,

legal system they do so either because they are *summoned by the public prosecution* and therefore are *forced* to do or because such procedures are the *last resort* if any of the other attempts to solve the dispute by means of alternative arbitration have failed. In other tribal nations that base their state ideology on Islam, such as Afghanistan, Pakistan and Somalia, we can detect similar tendencies.

3.5.5 *The executive power*

By the end of the 1970s a public prosecution system[25] (*al-niyaba al-'amma*) was introduced in Yemen, but in practice the victim still has to engage himself personally in order to have a case tried before the court. This requires, of course, private resources.[26] The Yemeni state is therefore not a public actor in the way we in Norway are familiar with, but rather an *intricate cohesion of economic and military elites* who co-operate with tribal leaders.[27] In order to prosecute someone one therefore actually has to have the *power* to do so. What unfolds during court proceedings is thus in many cases only a part of a long and complicated legal process, which can be taken in and out of the official court, depending on what suits the interests of the parties best. In such situations the judge is forced to favour influential parties. In the next section, Yemeni criminal law and the role of the state in the criminal procedure will be explored further.

'What is plural in the law? A praxiological answer,' *Le shaykh et le procureur*, 1 (2005); Léon Buskens, 'An Islamic Triangle: Changing Relationships between Shari'a, State Law and Local Customs,' *ISIM Review*, (2000), p. 8.

25 See Brinkley Messick, 'Prosecution in Yemen: The Introduction of the Niyaba', *International Journal of Middle East Studies*, 15 (1983), pp. 507–18.

26 Even if Article 21 of the Republican Decree No. 12 of 1994 Concerning Crimes and Penalties and Republican Decree concerning Law No. 13 of 1994 Concerning the Criminal Procedures states that '[the] General Prosecution has the jurisdiction over the initiation, presentation and implementation [of the criminal lawsuit] in the Court', Article 27 of the same law states that '[the] General Prosecution may not file charges before the Court except when it is based on complaint filed by the victim or anyone acting legally on his behalf.'

27 See Alley, 'The Rules of the Game', pp. 385–409.

3.6   Criminal law in Yemen: Balancing state legislation, Shari'a and private arbitration

3.6.1 Criminal law in Yemen

As mentioned above, modern criminal law in Yemen consists of a mixture of French, Egyptian and *Zaydi* law. At the same time, Yemeni criminal law contains elements of classical Islamic juris-prudence (*fiqh*), often simply referred to as the Shari'a by popular belief in the West, for certain types of crime.[28] As many prejudices concerning Islamic criminal law still exist, a brief explanation will be provided here first.

3.6.2 Hadd-punishments; crimes against religion

Classical Islamic criminal law can be divided into three separate categories: *hadd*, *qisas* and *ta'zir*. The *hadd* punishments cover only a little part of what in Western legal orders is defined as criminal law. *Hadd* crimes are first of all are perceived to be crimes against religion and the corresponding sentencing is therefore concretely prescribed by the Koran and the Sunna,[29] the prime legal sources of Islamic law. Classical Islamic law defines the following categories of crimes against religion:[30]

> (1) Theft, which is punishable with the amputation or the loss of a hand (*sariqah*);[31]

28   The burden of proof in cases punishable by the *hudud* is extensive. Even though the Yemeni penal code formally applies *hadd* (pl. *hudud*) punishments to certain types of crimes, these punishments are seldom applied in practice. See also An-Na'im, *Islamic Family Law in a Changing World*, p. 145.

29   The *Sunna* is a collection of the normative sayings and ways of behaviour by the Prophet Muhammad, often collected in narratives, which are called a *hadith*.

30   As elaborated by Rudolph Peters, these crimes against religion are usually termed *hudud*, but they are not entirely defined. See, for instance, Rudolph Peters, *Crime and Punishment in Islamic Law: Theory and Practice from the Sixteenth to the Twenty-First Century* (Cambridge University Press, 2005), pp. 6–68.

31   Pursuant to Koran 5. 37–38; See W. Heffening, 'Sarika', P. Bearman, Th. Bianquis, C.E. Bosworth, E. van Donzel and W.P. Heinrichs, (eds.), *Encyclopaedia of Islam*, 2nd edition (Leiden: Brill Online, 2010).

(2) Banditry[32] or armed robbery, which is punishable with the death penalty, crucifixion, cross-amputation of a hand or a foot or exclusion *(hirabah)*;[33]

(3) Unlawful sexual intercourse *(zina)*, which is punishable with 100 lashes *(zina)*;[34]

(4) False accusations of zina, which is punishable with 80 lashes *(qadf)*;[35]

(5) Apostasy from Islam *(ridda)*, which is punishable with the death penalty; and

(6) Consumption of alcohol, which is punishable with 80 lashes.[36]

It should be added, that although many of these rules are mentioned in the present Yemeni criminal law, they are rarely used presently and some prescribe imprisonment as punishment.

3.6.3 *Murder and bodily harm*

It follows therefore from the above that murder is therefore *not* punishable by means of *hudud* penalties. Classical Islamic law takes a fundamentally different approach to murder. As Islamic Law generally does not divide between public and private law, murder is not considered a part of public law, as in Western legal orders, but is rather deemed a part of private law *(haqq adami)*. Premeditated murder, voluntary manslaughter and assault are therefore classified in a separate category, as these criminal acts are punishable either with *retaliation (qisas)* or by means of a *monetary compensation (diyya)*. There is no prosecution or execution of sentence *ex officio*, just a guarantee of the right to retaliation. This implies that private retaliation or blood vengeance is not automatically allowed, but rather requires that vengeance takes place within the legal framework as set by Islamic law. Compensation is granted only in case the victim or the victim's relatives do not wish to make use of the possibility of retaliation, or if vengeance – for whatever reason – cannot take place.

---

32 Traditionally robbery.
33 See Koran 5. 33.
34 See Koran 24. 2.
35 See Koran 24. 4.
36 Abiad, *Sharia, Muslim States and International Human Rights Treaty Obligations*, pp. 4–5; Knut S. Vikør, *Between God and the Sultan: A History of Islamic Law* (London: Hurst & Company, 2005), pp. 280–87.

Furthermore, Islamic law requires that a Muslim judge, a *qadi*, will hear the parties' assertions. In order to be convicted, the criminal act needs to be witnessed by trustworthy witnesses. Islamic law is formalistic in the sense that it is based to a large extent on eyewitnesses, in particular with regard to the criminal acts punishable by *hudud*. As the *hudud* punishments are so severe, the burden of proof as provided by the eyewitnesses must be solid and not 'be beyond reasonable doubt' as in Norwegian criminal law. Each criminal act requires a certain number of witnesses.

3.6.4 *Ta'zir; discretion of the judge*

Ta'zir comprises all sentencing that does not fall under the category of the *hudud* or *qisas* and therefore can be determined at the judge's discretion. In modern Yemeni state legislation *ta'zir* punishments mainly take the form of imprisonment and provide guidelines for the severity of the punishments in the penal code.[37]

3.6.5 *Legal institutions for criminal procedure in Yemen*

Courts are situated in each district (*mudiriya*) of the country with jurisdiction in, *inter alia*, criminal affairs. Each governorate (*muhafaza*) also has its Courts of Appeal for criminal cases and the Supreme Court has a department of criminal affairs as well.[38] In practice, however, criminal procedure is relatively little practised in Yemen. High litigation costs, time-consuming trials and corruption have led to the fact that many prefer to solve their disputes by means of tribal and customary arbitration.

3.6.6 *Tribal and customary law ('urf)*

Even though both modern state legislation and classical Islamic law recognise that individuals are personally responsible for their own actions, tribal law and local customary law ('*urf*) also presume that the family, clan or the tribe collectively can be held responsible for serious criminal actions. Good relationships to one's family and kin

---

37   *Cf.* Republican Decree of Law No. 12 of 1994 Concerning Crimes and Penalties.
38   See An-Na'im, *Islamic Family Law in a Changing World*, p. 145.

are therefore of great importance in a country in which the police, social welfare system and the national health service functions quite differently from in Norway. In Yemen it is possible for the head of the family, normally the father, to contact the police to ask them to put a dissident son in prison for a couple of days. It is the head of the family who in agreement with the other male family members represents their common interests in the public sphere.

As a consequence, murder is *not only considered to be a crime against the individual or society at large, but rather a crime against another family, kin or tribe* in which there are two possible outcomes if sufficient proof and admission of guilt are accounted for: the first being blood vengeance and the other being a monetary compensation. The state becomes a part in murder cases only if the guilty party has offended the state directly, or if the murder is of an aggravating character in which public opinion becomes so strong that the state feels obliged to intervene.

In the case of a conflict between two individuals, the question of guilt and the claim for compensation is addressed not only to the individual himself, but to the whole family, clan or tribe of which the offender is a member. This collective responsibility is not restricted to criminal law only. It is thus important for the family or tribe to defend and support its members, while simultaneously striving to keep peace and order and maintain good relations with the other families or tribes in the area in order to minimise conflict.

3.6.7 Arbitration procedures

Such negotiations often take place in a way in which the offended party expresses towards the other party's family that he feels offended or dishonoured. In tribal cultures such a loss of honour can be given a physical expression by, for instance, planting a black flag near the other family's residence. The flag is interpreted by the counterpart as a way of expressing that 'the tribe's face is painted black' and as a consequence the whole tribe is dishonoured. The tribe will then do whatever is in its power to 'colour the flag white again'. Similarly, a wish for reconciliation can start with a public ritual slaughter of a bull in front of the victim's house. Yemeni tribes continue to follow the same negotiation patterns and principles today, also in murder cases, and Yemen is by no means unique in practising these negotiation mechanisms in conflict arbitration and the procedure described above is therefore to a large extent practised similarly in a much larger geographical area.[39]

The negotiations start with the mutual wish to find a solution upon which both parties can agree. During the negotiations, the offended party is represented by the head of the family, a lawyer, a secretary and several of the family's representatives. The offending party on the other hand is normally only represented by the perpetrator himself and a representative of his family. In addition, the parties choose a neutral judge in whom both families have confidence.[40] The judge's task is to hear the arguments made by the parties and finally to decide upon the amount of the compensation. Under any circumstances the perpetrator will accept the judge's decision and the compensation will be paid. This is because prior to negotiations the parties have to agree upon a kind of deposit, which will encourage them to accept the judgment. In minor cases this may be a dagger or a gun, which are important symbols for tribal membership and male identity in Yemen, in addition to being economically valuable. If the perpetrator cannot settle the account, the extended family, his clan or his tribe pays the deposit and the compensation. The perpetrator is then indebted to his family and tribe.

Negotiations often take place near the offended party's residence and both parties take the necessary time to settle the disagreement. Prior to negotiations all participants take off their weapons, mobile phones, jewellery or other status symbols. These status symbols will be returned by the judge only after the negotiations have ended. Sometimes the parties agree not to serve food during the negotiations in order to 'force' the parties to reach an agreement

39 See, for instance, Shelagh Weir, *A Tribal Order, Politics and Law in the Mountains of Yemen* (Austin: University of Texas Press, 2007), in general and specifically pp. 165–89. Further reference is made to the work of Frank Stewart, Professor at the Hebrew University of Jerusalem, who during many years has studied negotiation strategies among the Bedouin tribes in Israel, Egypt and Jordan. These forms of negotiation have also been documented on film by Uri Mintzker at the Ben Gurion University of the Negev as presented during a presentation called 'Tribal law of the Bedouin of the Negev' during the workshop 'Behind the Rule – Law and Identity, organised by the Graduate School Society and Culture in Motion at the Martin Luther University Halle–Wittenberg on 3 and 4 July 2009.

40 The Arabic word '*tahkim*' means to appoint (such a customary) judge who is then called a '*muhakkam*'.

more quickly.[41] On other occasions the parties agree that the perpetrator is financially responsible for the negotiation process, which may include having to cover the subsistence expenses of all the participating members. Such agreements may turn out to become an expensive affair once the negotiation process drags on too much.

3.6.8 Amount of compensation

The offended family will attempt to obtain the highest possible compensation in order to demonstrate the size of the family's loss. The imbalance between the two parties is re-established by means of monetary compensation. The actual size of monetary compensations has always varied much from case to case, even when such cases are taken into the state court system. In an attempt to determine a certain standard, the Yemeni Ministry of Justice has decided a fixed amount of compensation for murder (*diya*). In 2007, a decree was sent to the national courts stating that the compensation to be paid in case of murder is 5.5 million riyal (ca. USD 26,000) and for accidental killing 1.6 million riyal (ca. USD 8,000).[42] As for the actual implementation of this decree, information could not be found for the present study.

3.6.9 Restorative justice in murder cases in Yemen?

In this chapter we asked whether there are elements in the way in which murder cases are dealt with in Yemen that coincide with the Western idea of *restorative justice*. In Yemen the state does not automatically see it as its responsibility to engage itself in criminal cases that concern murder and bodily harm, as this generally is perceived to be a private affair. Still, the Yemeni state does offer a legal framework for how murder cases can be settled and how punishment can be applied. In case of murder and bodily harm the victim or the victim's relatives can choose between punishment

---

41 According to Frank Stewart who himself has experience as a judge in such negotiations – see the penultimate footnote.

42 See: Public notifications and decrees and certification of notaries, No. 6 of 2007 concerning the following of Law No. 32 of 2006, Regarding updating the size of compensation for murder and bodily harm, p. 13, Ministry of Justice, Republic of Yemen.

and compensation.

If the Yemeni state cannot offer a satisfactory solution within the formal framework of state legislation, the only option for the victim or his or her relatives is to accept a solution based on a monetary compensation. Obviously, strong parties will in such procedures have more possibilities to obtain a higher compensation than weaker ones. A weaker party in Yemen is therefore not guaranteed the same form of legal protection and legal certainty as the stronger party. Such an arbitration-based system therefore functions best in cases where the parties have a somewhat equal social status.

Yemeni criminal law and the way it is practised in current Yemeni society may seem strange to Western eyes. The fact that the state does not have a legal monopoly on punishment, but opens up the possibility of private arbitration and negotiation that in some cases may even result into blood vengeance, is unacceptable within a Western *Rechtsstaat*.[43] The fact that a victim or the victims family can play a more active role in addition to the state in criminal cases may open up the possibility of injustice. Obviously, this infringes the principles of equality before the law and fundamental human rights, such as, for instance, the right to a fair trail.

However, even though the Yemeni system may seem defective, it also may have its positive aspects. Victims and their relatives are given a much larger role in the criminal procedures themselves. In addition, the Yemeni system permits arbitration and reconciliation between the two parties. In many Western criminal justice systems the victims have traditionally been excluded to a significant degree as parts of the process. As a result, victims and their relatives often feel disregarded and some wish to be included to a much larger extent in the legal procedures initiated by the state. The role of the victim in the criminal procedures is emphasised in the theories about 'restorative justice' as a positive aspect that helps the victim and the victim's relatives to put the case behind them and continue with their lives. These are elements that restorative justice and Islamic law as practised in criminal law in Yemen have in common.

43 See footnote 2, Chapter 1.

3.7 Some concluding thoughts

By presenting and clarifying Yemeni criminal law practices and how these practices are closely related to the social and cultural context, some fundamental questions can be posed, on a theoretical level, on the issue of non-state local conflict resolutions. The criminal law practices in Yemen and the way serious crime is handled by society have some fundamental resemblances with the concept of restorative justice as currently discussed within the Western legal context.

The victim and the victim's family play a more active role in the criminal process and can feel 'ownership' over the conflict. They may feel that they are listened to and taken seriously by the perpetrator, who by initiating negotiations signalises an intention to restore the imbalance between the parties. This implies that the perpetrator pleads guilty to the crime. In addition the arbitration process will lead to a form for compensation for the harm done. This may give the victim and the victim's relatives an opportunity to reconcile themselves with the thought that the injustice, although not completely restored, is compensated in a way that both parties can live with.

However, there are differences between restorative justice processes in Muslim and Western societies as well. Instead of a strong state that voluntarily gives away power in order to empower the victims as in case of restorative justice, as practiced in the West, the Yemeni inclination toward arbitration and private conflict resolution is more the result of the *absence* of a strong state. This vacuum has been filled by other historical, political, social and cultural structures and elements. Additionally, the social and cultural context within which the parties arbitrate is fundamental to how any given conflict can be settled and the parties must share a certain minimum of expectations of what is perceived as correct justice. For instance, in Yemen the parties choose an arbitrator in whom they both have confidence. This arbitrator will go to considerable length to reconcile the parties, not only to keep the peace and order between the tribes, but also in order to protect the arbitrator's own reputation as a mediator and an arbitrator. This presupposition, securing the function of the arbitrator, may be lacking in, for instance, a Western restorative justice setting where the arbitrator usually is appointed by, and is representing, the state.

These aspects make the function of elements of restorative justice an essentially different concept in Yemen from in Western criminal law. It also gives reason to question the future of restorative justice, both in its current expression in Yemen and as a future means for conflict resolution within Western societies.

Restorative justice does to a certain degree necessarily imply a 'localisation' and 'personification' of the conflict, but also the use of local and even personal symbols, ideas and standards of justice. In a small-scale face-to-face society, restoration of justice may be necessary for the actors to regain a normal, peaceful village life. However, if one of the parties belongs to another community outside the village or comes from a powerful elite, the outcome will favour the stronger part. A further consequence if the parties come from different parts of society or different geographical areas is that the parties and the arbitrator must make use of concepts, words and values in the arbitration process that are not necessarily shared by both parties to the arbitration. This aspect also becomes a potential future problem for restorative justice methods in both Yemen and in Western countries: Western states are no longer homogenous societies; internationalisation of society has made it more common that people travel abroad for holidays, work and education. The problem becomes even more pressing when the persons involved in the conflict at stake come from states in which one has different understandings of crime, guilt and justice, such as in Yemen.

To what extent there is a future for restorative justice in Yemen and/or in Western countries is a complex question that we shall not attempt to answer here. The core point that we have pointed to, with the use of Yemen as an example, is that the local social and cultural context of the criminal law to a certain degree determines the options of the actors involved in the (restorative) process and this makes it difficult to identify the legal processes themselves without also identifying the context. To understand the potential, and the costs and benefits of restorative justice as a solution, knowledge is needed of the local context of the specific conflict, not only of the formal legal context at the level of the national state.

References

Abiad, N., *Sharia, Muslim States and International Human Rights Treaty Obligations: A Comparative Study* (London: British Institute of International and Comparative Law (BIICL), 2008).

Alley, A.L., 'The Rules of the Game: Unpacking Patronage Politics in Yemen', *The Middle East Journal*, Vol. 64, No. 3, 25 (Summer 2010), pp. 385–409.

Andenæs, J., *Allminnelig strafferett* (Oslo: Akademisk forlag, 1956).

Buskens, L., 'An Islamic Triangle: Changing Relationships between Shari'a, State Law and Local Customs,' *ISIM Review*, (2000), p. 8.

Christie, N., 'Conflicts as Property', *The British Journal of Criminology*, 17 (1) (1977), pp. 1–15.

'Konflikt som eiendom', *TfR*, (1977), pp. 113–32.

'Conflicts as Property', in Andrew von Hirsch and Andrew Ashworth, *Principled Sentencing: Readings on Theory and Policy*, 2nd edition (Oxford: Hart Publishing, 1998), pp. 300–61.

Dupret, B., 'Legal Pluralism, Normative Plurality, and the Arab World,' in Baudouin Dupret, Maurits Berger and Laila al-Zwaini, (eds.), *Legal Pluralism in the Arab World* (The Hague, London, Boston: Kluwer Law International, 1999).

'What is plural in the law? A praxiological answer,' *Le shaykh et le procureur*, 1 (2005).

Heffening, W., 'Sarika', Bearman, P., Bianquis, T., Bosworth, C.E., Donzel, E. van, and Heinrichs, W.P., (eds.), *Encyclopaedia of Islam*, 2nd edition (Leiden: Brill Online, 2010).

Jacobsen, J., 'Diskusjonen om allmennprevensjonen sin faktiske verknad', *Tidsskrift for strafferett*, 4 (2004), pp. 394–438.

Fragment til forståing av den rettsstatlege strafferetten (Bergen: Fagbokforlaget, 2009).

Jansen Frederiksen, K., *Grensproblematiek tussen Saoedi-Arabie en Jemen: 'Asir, Najran en Jizan; een case study* ('Border disputes between Saudi Arabia and Yemen: 'Asir, Najran and Jizan: a case study') (University of Leiden Press, 1996).

Jansen Frederiksen, K., and Hovden, E., 'Jemenittisk strafferett: en intrikat blanding av nasjonal statslovgivning, islamsk rett og strafferett', ('Yemeni Criminal Law: an Intricate Mixture of National State Law, Islamic law and Criminal Law'), *Tidsskrift for Strafferett*, 2 (2010), pp. 154–68.

Marshall, T.F., *Restorative Justice: an Overview* (London: [British] Home Office, Research and Statistics Directorate, 1999).

Messick, B., 'Prosecution in Yemen: The Introduction of the Niyaba', *International Journal of Middle East Studies*, 15 (1983), pp. 507–18.

An-Na'im, A.A., (ed.), *Islamic Family Law in a Changing World. A Global Resource Book* (London: Zed Books Ltd, 2002).

Peters, R., *Crime and Punishment in Islamic Law: Theory and Practice from the Sixteenth to the Twenty-First Century* (Cambridge University Press, 2005), pp. 6–68.

Robberstad, A., *Mellom tvekamp og inkvisjon: straffeprosessens grunn-struktur belyst ved fornærmedes stilling* (Oslo: Universitetsforlaget, 1999).

Van Hoecke, M., 'Deep Level Comparative Law', in Mark Van Hoecke, (ed.), *Epistemology and Methodology of Comparative Law* (Oxford: Hart Publishing, 2004), pp. 165–95.

Vikør, K.S., *Between God and the Sultan: A History of Islamic Law* (London: Hurst & Company, 2005).

Weir, S., *A Tribal Order, Politics and Law in the Mountains of Yemen* (Austin: University of Texas Press, 2007).

Würth, A., *As-Sari'a fi Bab al-Yaman, Recht, Richter und Rechtpraxis an der familienrechtlichen Kammer des Gerichts Süd-Sanaa, (Republik Jemen) 1983-1995* (Berlin: Duncker and Humblot, 2000).

'Stalled Reform: Family Law in Post-Unification Yemen', *Islamic Law and Society*, 12 (2003), pp. 12–33.

al-Zwaini, L., 'Mediating between Custom and Code: Dar al-Salam, an NGO for Tribal Arbitration in Sanaa', *Monde Arabe*, 1 (2005).

Legal sources

INTERNATIONAL COVENANTS

International Covenant on Civil and Political Rights (ICCPR)

International Covenant on Economic, Social and Cultural Rights (ICESCR).

NORWAY

NOU 2002: 4

YEMEN

The Yemeni Constitution of 1994 (in English, see http://www.al-bab.com/yemen/gov/con94.htm).

The Republican Decree No. 12 of 1994 Concerning Crimes and Penalties (In English translation: http://www.unhcr.org/refworld/country/YEM.html).

The Republican Decree Concerning Law No. 13 of 1994 Concerning the Criminal Procedures (In English translation: http://www.unhcr.org/refworld/country/YEM.html).

The Arbitration Act (in Arabic only: *Qanun al-tahkim*). Republican Decree 22 of 1992.

The Personal Status Law of Republican Decree No. 20 of 1992 (In Arabic only. *Qanun al-ahwal al-shakhsiyya*).

The Yemeni Civil Code, No. 19 of 1992 (in Arabic: *Qanun al-Madani*).

Public notifications and decrees and certification of notaries, No. 6 of 2007 concerning the following of Law No. 32 of 2006, Regarding updating the size of compensation by murder and bodily harm (in Arabic only): *Ta'mim raqam 6 li-sanat 2007, bi-sha'n tatbiq al-qanun raqam 32 li-sanat 2006 al-khass bi-ta'dil miqdar al-diyya wa-l-arsh. al-ta'amim wa-l-qarrarat wa tarakhis al-umana li-'amm 2007.*

4. Victims of inconclusive criminal evidence against offenders

State liability and some more restorative semi-remedies

HENDRIK KAPTEIN

4.1 Introduction

The ever increasing role of victims in criminal justice and its less formal offshoots in mediation and the like are a good thing in principle. Something is done for victims of crime at last – which of course is not to say that such victims were previously completely abandoned.

Indeed, in several 'civilised' jurisdictions, restorative justice has made some inroads into the realms of criminal justice recently. Since about 1980 mediation has replaced formal proceedings to some extent, sometimes even in cases of serious crime like grievous bodily harm and rape. Such mediation may forestall indictment, or formal indictment may lead to court orders against criminal defendants to participate in mediation, pay damages and/or offer other kinds of redress and compensation as part of mediation processes. If there still is a criminal case at court, victims may not just testify, but also speak out, in terms of victim impact statements. Additionally, they may sue for damages in criminal proceedings. Furthermore, they may ask courts to order public prosecution offices to indict suspects, just as courts may sentence defendants to additional measures such as staying away from victims. Such and more reforms may at least offer some comfort to victims of crime, though not all consequences of crime may be done away with by this of course.[1]

---

1   For a reasonably recent overview, and also on international criminal law, see
     G. Johnstone and D.W. Van Ness, *Handbook of Restorative Justice*, (Cullompton,
     Devon, UK: Willan Publishing, 2006.) On older developments see S. Schafer,
     Compensation and Restitution to Victims of Crime [1960], (Montclair, NJ: Patterson
     Smith, 1970).

None the less, as is well known, the procedural and/or material introduction of the rights of victims of crime and their interests into criminal justice does not proceed without more than occasional hiccups and even principled opposition. Criminal law has essentially been public law for centuries, at least in so-called civilised jurisdictions as exemplified in Europe, Northern America, Australia and elsewhere. Civil law, incorporating tort law, was long conceived as the one and only formal instrument for victims of crime seeking redress. Whether the practice of civil law and procedure generally satisfied such victims of crime is another matter of course.

More specifically, it has been suggested that criminal justice concerns only the relationships of the state and (potential) criminal defendants. The realisation of law and order is the function of criminal law, procedure and punishment, and nothing else. Victims of crime have nothing to do with this. Introduction of such third parties reduces principled wholes of criminal law and criminal procedure to patchworks, to the detriment of public purposes. Also, feigned or even real solidarity with victims of crime may contribute to ever harsher punishment, not at all mitigated by the return of retribution as the core justification of punishment, at least in public and political opinion, or so it is contended.

Problems of evidence and proof relating to increasing roles of victims in criminal proceedings are probably less extensively discussed. Thus orthodoxy had it that criminal standards of proof ought to be strict. One reason for this is the real evil of punishing the innocent, compared with the marginal loss of general interest by letting guilty defendants go free. Or, as long as a sufficient number of offenders is punished, public interest may still be adequately served, even if some guilty defendants go free. This holds good as long as criminal justice is to serve general interests only. Punishing even one innocent defendant, however, is a violation of a basic right. Thus *in dubio abstine* is the principle. Whether this is lived by is another matter of course.

Victims of crime as third parties in criminal proceedings lead to complications here as well. Marginal doubts about relevant evidence may lead to the acquittal of criminal defendants in conflicts with the state representing general interests only. However, acquittal on the basis of such marginal doubts may wrong the victims of crime. In criminal proceedings intended to serve the public interest, criminal defendants are the primary stakeholders in terms of rights. Any introduction of restorative justice, on the other hand, leads to a second category of participants entitled to relevant rights: victims of crime.

This produces an interesting dilemma. Safeguarding defendants' rights to adequate standards of proof may lead to a violation of victims' rights. Conversely, trying to do justice to victims of crime may threaten adequate standards of proof. This problem may not be limited to formal criminal conflict resolution. Any issue of possible offender v. real victim (or even possible victim), however informal, may lead to the same problem. In the end nothing more may be left than 'one person's word against another's'.

Some consolation may be found in the fact that about 90 per cent of criminal cases are decided upon on the basis of indubitable evidence of sorts, at least in so-called civilised jurisdictions. Additionally, more than a few of such doubtful cases relate to public interest violations only and thus have nothing to do with specific victims. So the problem of standards of proof favouring criminal defendants and not serving victims of crime may not be huge, at least from a statistical point of view.

Nevertheless, individual cases – however rare one may well hope against better knowledge – may show the dramatic side of things. For example, a woman arrives at a police station, in a state of utter bewilderment, showing all the signs of having been raped. She appears to be certain about the identity of the offender; DNA-testing points to the same person having been near to the supposed victim. The suspect, or even defendant, retorts, 'Yes, I was there, but come on, she liked the sex, I did not really force her to do anything.' In the end the (highest) court refuses to sentence, as the evidence available is still compatible with a more or less voluntary scenario, given not totally implausible but contradictory versions of the facts as told by the different persons directly concerned. (Such issues may not be completely alleviated by redefinition of offences in terms of less strict criminal intent and/or guilt and/or due care, as exemplified in the Norwegian penal code, § 192 section 4, concerning gross negligent rape, though such broader concepts may indeed lead to more offenders being taken to task, restoratively or otherwise.)

Thus the rather very small risk of sentencing an innocent person is avoided, by leaving the possible very real victim out in the cold. One well-known reason why real victims may stay traumatised is their common conviction that they were guilty themselves in the end, as no official and authoritative 'transfer of guilt to the real offender' has been effected after all.

Insufficient evidence and proof may also be the simple and conclusive consequence of potential criminal defendants not even having been identified, let alone arrested. Too many victims have to live in the knowledge that offenders, having harmed them, go free without ever having been bothered by any criminal proceedings.

So indeed issues of standards of proof to be discussed here may not be of overwhelming importance in comparative respects. Still marginalia as sketched here may lead to ways out of the 'standards of proof' dilemma in principle, and have meaningful implications for victims of unsolved crime in general.

Thus Section 4.2 offers a brief sketch of theoretical and some practical limitations of evidence and proof as directed at the establishment of historical realities relevant to criminal charges and convictions. Bentham's ideas are revived once again, in order to show that any unconditional or even 'absolute' certainty about the past on the basis of any evidence presently available is a will-o'-the-wisp. However, in criminal proceedings serving public and general interests only this is no real problem. Strict standards of proof that minimise the risks of doing injustice to innocent defendants may indeed still lead to general interests being sufficiently well served, as long as sufficient levels of sentencing and punishment are upheld. Alternatively, no stakeholder in criminal proceedings is entitled to any right to involvement in sentencing and punishment. Doubts about the legitimation of punishment as the infliction of pain may also lead to still greater strictness in standards of proof in principle. The less punishment there is on doubtful moral grounds, the better (Section 4.3).

Section 4.4, however, purports to explain why victims of crime as stakeholders complicate this principled world, as their rights may be wronged by the acquittal of defendants whom such victims may have every right to believe really harmed them. On the other hand, standards of proof protecting defendants, however *mala fide*, may really wrong victims of crime. 'Civilisation' of evidence law in criminal proceedings may seem the natural solution. Proof may no longer be something like the scientific establishment of criminally relevant pasts on the basis of presently available evidence in principle, but the result of a strictly regulated contest of the parties concerned, on the basis of different 'stories' of the case at hand. A reform of criminal evidence law to the style of civil proceedings would not be a good thing, however strong current tendencies toward it may be (Section 4.5).

A rather different and probably more satisfactory remedy would be compensation and restitution by state funds for victims wronged by acquittal on the basis of strict standards of proof as well. Also, some victims' satisfaction may be derived from the state accepting full liability for not having prevented victimisation in the first place. This may be a sensible consequence of criminal justice as public law (Section 4.6). In the end, however, no really satisfactory solution seems at hand. There is no alternative to strict criminal standards of proof anyway. Current criminal justice and its practice may be less important for victims of crime than so many other good things to be done to them (Section 4.7).

4.2 Reconstructing the past: The margins of uncertainty

The past is the past, irretrievably gone – as long as time travel in any backward direction according to theories of relativity remains an impossibility, given that entropy blocks backward motion in principle and given that there are probably some practical limitations as well. Philosophers even deny the existence of the past. According to the fashionable philosophy of presentism, actual reality is the one and only reality. Even if such a stance may be regarded as rather too philosophical, all that remains of the past are bits and pieces of evidence pointing in one way or another to how this past may have been, or may not have been.

Additionally, there is the human tendency to collect evidence with an eye to expected or even desired outcomes. Thus police officials tend to look for corroborating evidence, possibly overlooking other evidence contradicting the charge in question. Adding to this are further deficiencies in fact-finding or even *mala fide* selection of evidence. Then there are so many intractable problems with witnesses, even if they are really trying to be completely honest. Criminal defendants and victims may contradict each other without there being any real clarity on who is more faithful to the facts of the case.

'But not all evidence is circumstantial!' it will be countered. There may be direct or even immediate evidence available, like dented cars, forged documents or even wounded victims in the courtroom, or so it is contended. Remember, however, that any distinction between direct and indirect criminal evidence relates to the final decisive body, that is, the court. ('Court' is shorthand here for any finally decisive official bodies on facts of criminal charges. Hence, possible jury roles in the establishment of criminal evidence and proof are not discussed separately here.) What then remains of really direct evidence? Not much it may seem, maybe apart from marginal cases like perjury. But even such perjury presupposes contrary knowledge not based solely on direct evidence.

A fourfold distinction of kinds of evidence is apposite here.

Firstly, there may indeed be direct evidence, available to the court 'as such', however rare such evidence may be in practice.

Secondly, and more common, is indirect or circumstantial evidence, here briefly defined as any evidence possibly explained by the facts of the charge. Thus there may be a dead body, with a knife next to it carrying both the deceased person's blood and the criminal defendant's fingerprints. Facts of charges like murder or manslaughter against this defendant may explain the evidence available. However, there may be alternative explanations for the same evidence excluding the facts of such a charge, like a neighbour having stolen the knife and having committed the crime instead.

Thirdly, there may be testimonial evidence of facts of charges themselves. Thus a witness may tell the court: 'I am dead certain that this man crossed the road while the traffic light was red.' All kinds of error may creep in here, as is of course amply documented. Also, any relevant *mens rea* is not directly observable in principle, as outward human movement needs to be interpreted in terms of intentions, motives, and/or superior inner and/or outer forces in order to classify such movements as conduct or even deliberate conduct. This may be no problem at all in normal social intercourse, inconceivable as it is without the know-how of normal interpretation and explanation of more or less standard rule-governed behaviour. But this may be precisely the problem of the default interpretation of outward movement in terms of intentional facts of charges, as such default interpretation or in fact abductive explanation (the basic structure of which is to be explained shortly) may still be wrong, at the expense of factually innocent criminal defendants, who may then face rather worse consequences than just being misunderstood in daily life and communication. So still no facts of charges relating to motives and deliberation in general, or the absence of such facts, may be based on any direct testimonial evidence.

Fourthly, and probably most important, is the testimonial evidence of circumstantial evidence. This ranges from crime scene bystanders' observations or better: memories to forensic specialists' reports and interpretations of (hopefully) scientific research relating to the case. However scientifically sound, such forensic evidence does not constitute conclusive evidence in itself either.

Related to this sobering fourfold distinction is the indirect relationship of facts of charges to any observable natural or institutional reality. Thus a witness may reliably testify about bodily movements of a defendant, followed by another person falling to the ground. Even in such relatively simple cases, commonsense concepts of natural observation need to be translated into concepts of material criminal law, like grievous bodily harm. Or institutional realities like banknotes may be seen to have been handed over, possibly coming down to money-laundering, blackmailing and/or corruption. Again, such qualifications presuppose translation of some or other observed reality into the language of material criminal law. Thus there is no direct evidence for this reason as well. (Compare this with interpretive issues concerning *mens rea* and the like as noted before.)

So the truth of the matter is to be reconstructed on such shallow bases. Law-like statements of any general plausibility are needed to link possible remains of the past with parts of the past itself. Thus a bruised face may relate to grievous bodily harm on the basis of general knowledge causally linking disturbed facial states to bodily contact with other persons. Motivational laws may be apposite as well, such as somebody illegally and forcibly entering a shop may well be after money and/or other valuables. Not all of such general causal and motivational laws transcend rule-of-thumb status. Also remember criminal evidence and proof are related to specific, individual facts in principle, not to generic or even general facts and knowledge – though such generic and general knowledge may of course be useful in linking evidence to facts of charges. So general methods of confirmation, corroboration, falsification and prediction are inapplicable in principle.

In fact the basic logical structure of linking evidence to facts of charges is abductive (already briefly alluded to regarding imputation of motives). Put in propositional or 'baby logic' form this comes down to the following:

$$p \rightarrow q$$
$$q$$
$$\overline{}$$
$$p$$

Or: if p (any proposition, like 'It is raining'), then q (any other proposition, as an implication of p, like 'The streets are wet'), q, so p.

This is not good logic of course, confusing necessary and sufficient conditions, though it may be the one most common implicit structure in argumentation. 'Default explanation' is what is lived by as long as there is no better explanation available and as long as havoc does not ensue.[2]

Abductive relationships of criminal evidence to facts of a charge are of the following structure:

facts of charge $\rightarrow$ evidence concerned

evidence concerned

$$\overline{}$$

facts of charge

Or (for example): if Paul killed Peter in the garden (simplified facts of charge), then Peter's dead body was to be found in that same garden (evidence), Peter's body was found in the garden, so Paul killed Peter.

If the evidence concerned is reliable in itself and if causal and motivational laws explaining the implication are plausible or even true, then the facts of the charge may be shown to offer an

2   See H.J.R. Kaptein, H. Prakken and B. Verheij, (eds.), Legal Evidence and
     Proof: Statistics, Stories, Logic (Farnham: Ashgate Publishing Limited, 2009).

adequate explanation of the available evidence. But this is no good, as alternative explanations of the same evidence may be available, relating to facts incompatible with the facts of the charge. Thus the same bruised face may have been caused by grievous bodily harm, but also by some or other accident. Or, abductive logic may lead to acceptable conclusions – again given reliable evidence and plausible general laws linking evidence to the facts of the charge – but only if all possible alternative explanations are shown to be inapplicable in the case at hand.

A daunting task indeed. Probably the best way to exclude all alternative explanations is to prove alibis conclusively for all other possible actors and in fact for all other possible causes. In fact the elementary logic of alibis, *modus tollens*, is rather better than abductive logic:

$$p \rightarrow q$$
$$\neg q$$
___
$$\neg p$$

Or,

facts of a charge $\rightarrow$ some or other implication of them
$\neg$ (any implication)

___

$\neg$ (facts of charge)

'$\neg$' = 'non-', indicates denial of the proposition concerned

Thus a criminal defendant charged with murdering his mother by shooting a ballpoint pen through her eyeball by means of a crossbow may conclusively exonerate himself by pointing to the proven impossibility of an implication of this charge, of any ballpoint-like thing penetrating an eyeball if propelled by not much stronger force than is possibly produced by any crossbow.[3]

This is one way to explain the asymmetry of proving a defendant's innocence on the basis of an alibi, and proving the facts of the charge on the other hand. An alibi may be so strong as not

---

3   Interested readers may consult M. Malsch and J.F. Nijboer (eds.), *Complex Cases: Perspectives on the Netherlands Criminal Justice System* (Amsterdam: Thela Thesis, 1999) on this bizarre case, which yet again shows that not all courts are sufficiently able to understand such argumentation in any due time.

to leave room for any reasonable doubt, whereas proof of facts of charges will never have the same certainty – at least not on the basis of any abductive reasoning implying the need to exclude every alternative explanation.

But this is too strict, adherents of probability reasoning in matters of criminal evidence and proof will retort. Probability theory has been hard science for almost a century now, so why not make good use of such theory in excluding any reasonable doubt? Its axioms may indeed be beyond doubt, but nevertheless apart from different conceptions of probability theory itself (like fashionable Bayesian subjectivism versus frequentism), applied probability theory is more of a minefield than anything really useful. Even if it were not, too many court members and other officials involved lack any basic understanding of probability theory and its applications.

Thus in one infamous criminal case in the Netherlands, a former nurse was convicted to a life sentence on the basis of the presumably extreme unlikelihood of natural or at least normal causes of a number of deaths in her immediate professional vicinity. It took several years before it dawned on the Supreme Court of the Netherlands that both the statistics and their application in this specific case were botched.[4] This is just one example of problems not only in this case: statistical correlation does not imply any causal relationship by itself, which of course is the infamous fallacy of *cum hoc ergo propter hoc*.

Probably the main reason why any probability theory, however mathematically and scientifically sound in itself, is not applicable to criminal evidence and proof is the qualitative complexity of human conduct. Probability theory is about quantities only in principle. Even the – hopefully limited – sphere of human conduct relevant for criminal justice far surpasses any possible quantitative description and explanation. Remember that material criminal law refers to the implicit or sometimes explicit complexity of human conduct and its consequences. This holds good both for presumed probabilities of unique historical events such as facts of charges, and for any causal and/or motivational general laws purporting to

4   On comparable cases in the United Kingdom and elsewhere see T. Derksen and M. Meijsing, 'The Fabrication of Facts: The Lure of the Incredible Coincidence' in Kaptein, Prakken and Verheij, (eds.), *Legal Evidence and Proof*.

explain such human conduct. No semblance of scientific certainty in probabilistic reasoning can ignore this basic given. So there is nothing like exclusion of reasonable doubt about the basis of anything like 'extremely small quantitative likelihood of innocence', that is, even if it were denied that any quantifiable probability, however small, that any criminal defendant is innocent after all ought to lead to acquittal.

So unclear uncertainties of abductive logic are still to be lived with. Argumentation on the reliability of testimonies is at least partly abductive and thus logically defective as well. One reason why a witness may tell the court that the criminal defendant assaulted her may be that it really happened. There may be other reasons, motives or causes for the very same testimony as well, ranging from *bona fide* mistaken identity to malicious collaboration with other 'witnesses' in order to get an innocent defendant convicted. In addition, judging testimonies relies on argumentation *ad hominem* in principle. Remember no witnesses would be needed if there were any independent access to facts concerned. But then such argumentation *ad hominem* is notoriously unreliable, if not even outright fallacious, not just because witnesses may lie in court without at all giving this away to any observer.

Motives or the absence of them are important for determining guilt of criminal defendants as well. Even if the facts of charges in terms of criminal conduct are conclusively established, there may still be different possible explanations for such conduct. Thus indubitable killing may be explained in terms of completely unhindered deliberation, or exclusively in terms of causes to be explained by forensic psychiatry, or in terms of all kinds of mixes of both. Apart from varieties of petty crime there may be no criminal conviction without *mens rea* in principle of course (though of course involuntary criminal conduct may lead to other measures against the defendants concerned). Again, abductive logic and its pitfalls loom large here. Here not much stronger reasoning is found than in the use of motivational laws in order to try first to find out what happened.

Circular reasoning may be the result, as in the case against the nurse. Thus it was reasoned against her that her motives must have been really *mala fide*, or she would not have committed such cruelty against these patients. Such motives in their turn were conceived as further corroboration of her crimes. One public prosecution officer even stated against her that her *mala fide* motives were beyond any doubt, as she had taken care not to leave any trace of her crimes (!). Such really harmful fallacies – wrapped in legal slang and its false semblance of authority – may go unnoticed all too often.

Even apart from such fallaciousness and outright stupidity, criminal fact-finding resembles archeology and historiography more than hard science. Archeology is to be found in the reconstruction of uncertain criminal pasts in terms of remains still available in the courtroom. Historiography tries to explain motives and/ or causes behind historical events well established in themselves. The same structure is to be found in the imputation of motives and/ or explanation in terms of causes behind proven criminal conduct. As in real archeology and historiography, no more than interesting mixes of speculation and some science may be expected. This may not be a bad thing in academic science and scholarship about the past, leading to interesting conflicts on the history of mankind, but it is probably not a nice perspective for any innocent criminal defendants unable to prove conclusively that they have been wrongly charged or even convicted.

In fact the establishment of criminal evidence and proof may be nothing much more than the story-telling, still further remote from the scientific aspects of archeology and historiography. Police and public prosecution officials, defendants, victims, witnesses and others concerned have their so often conflicting stories 'of what really happened and why'. Stories do not create their own truth, in so far as they can be tested against any independent reality at all if facts of criminal charges are concerned. So in the end the court creates its own story of what really happened and why, without any clearly demonstrable relationships to relevant pasts. But stories do not constitute proof, in any minimal sense of derivation of innocence or guilt in terms of facts of charges on the basis of reliable evidence and relevant science.[5]

This of course is only a small part of the whole story – if there may be anything like it at all – depicting so many theoretical and practical limitations in establishing criminally relevant pasts on the

5   W.A. Wagenaar, P.J. van Koppen and H.F.M. Crombag, *Anchored Narratives: The Psychology of Criminal Evidence* (Hemel Hempstead, Hertfordshire, UK: Harvester Wheatsheaf, and New York: St. Martin's Press, 1993).

basis of any remaining evidence. Also, and again, this is still apart from the hideous amount of avoidable mistakes, real stupidities and *mala fide* establishment of evidence and proof even in so-called civilised jurisdictions.

Commonsense has it that the past is the past and that the future is uncertain, or at least open. Apart from philosophical queries concerning the very existence of any past and future it may be best to give up this asymmetry and take it that the past is no more certain than the future. Strange as this may seem, it may be the one and only rational stance concerning evidence of human conduct in so far as is relevant for criminal justice.

Some readers may well have become rather impatient with this sceptical story by now. 'Is this to imply that there will be no more convictions, as there may be nothing like sufficient certainty about the past, criminal or otherwise? Come on, in so many cases we really know what happened, so please stop this doubtful academic exercise serving no worldly purpose.' Part of the answer is already to be found in the fact that about 90 per cent of criminal cases relate to reasonably indubitable facts of charges, based on confessions adequately tested in terms of criminal defendants' detailed knowledge of facts of the charge and other evidence (again, in so-called civilised jurisdictions only). Remember, however, that these doubts about the evidence and proof are all about the remaining 10 per cent or something like it: statistically insignificant perhaps, but still of possibly overwhelming importance to defendants, victims and others concerned. And please keep in mind as well that any '90 per cent safe versus 10 per cent doubtful' distinctions here do not exclude real possibilities of innocent criminal defendants being wrongly relegated to the 'safe' 90 per cent category.

4.3 *In dubio abstine?* How criminal justice serving public interests may accommodate high standards of proof

So if the innocent are to go free, every criminal case not leading to indubitable proof of the facts of the charge ought to lead to acquittal. 'Beyond reasonable doubt' standards, however differently formulated in different jurisdictions, ought to be interpreted in strict fashion. There ought to be no convictions on the basis of any probability implying that facts of charges might have been committed but that things might still have been otherwise. Sometimes grim realities of criminal trial and conviction of the innocent tell a different story of course, but this is hardly an argument against unconditional strictness of standards.

Probably more unsettling is the unconditional certainty that strictness of standards leads to less conviction in principle. The less room there is for doubt, the more offenders will go free. But this is nothing special, it may be retorted: so many offenders are not even caught, let alone brought to court. Apart from requirements of proportionality and subsidiarity in the deployment of forceful means according to criminal proceedings, public means are limited in principle and may not all be spent on handling the consequences of crime in terms of trial and punishment. Public interest is to be served and this amounts to more than trying to give all offenders their dues. *Fiat justitia pereat mundus* is not very practicable anyway (as is of course stated in this very same principle).

Or, as long as there is a sufficient general level of punishment serving public interests, offenders going free for whatever reasons are not a major problem. Some of these reasons may amount to no more than unavailability of public means to do criminal justice in specific cases or even classes of cases. One probably more plausible reason to let possible offenders go free is lack of certainty regarding their presumed misdeeds. So, indeed: *in dubio abstine*, even if this would imply leaving all of about 10 per cent of doubtful cases alone. Or so goes the theory in conceptions of criminal law as public law.

Does this put a premium on perfect crime, such as: the better offenders conceal their possibly capital misdeeds, the less likely they are to be convicted? Hardly, so one would think. Also, perfection in crime, or approximation of it, is not just the result of careful planning and execution, but also of less than perfect police investigation afterwards. Not all serious and capital crime is in the '10 per cent doubtful' category anyway.

Strict retributivism (*fiat justitia*... and the like) will indeed not accommodate this. If offenders have a right to be punished, just as all others are rightfully entitled to punishment against all offenders, then all exceptions to deserved punishment are wrong in principle. But even uncompromisingly strict varieties of retributivism will probably not be so fanatical as to willingly take the risk of condemning the innocent to undeserved punishment. Remember retributivism is about desert in the first place. Or punishing the innocent is to be taken as no better or worse than letting offenders deserving punishment go free. If this really is an implication of strict retributivism, then such justification of punishment must be deeply implausible anyway, even apart from so many more good reasons against it.[6]

Punishment for preventive purposes, probably more in line with serving general interests than strict retributivism, brings to light the relevant asymmetry still more clearly. Any slight reduction of numbers of punishments may lead to nothing worse than marginally less preventive effect (apart from clear and present dangers created by letting dangerous individuals go free). Thus lack of conclusive evidence may lead to leaving possibly criminal offenders alone. Punishing the innocent, however, is a violation of the basic right not to be sanctioned for anything not committed at all. This right may be part of any conception of crime and punishment. Strict consequentialism, in so far as plausible at all, may be one exception here, denying as it does the very idea of basic rights trumping interests. However, even the staunchest of consequentialists would probably attach at least some negative value to the public fear of being punished when innocent.

Thus any balancing leads to letting doubtful cases alone. No basic right to freedom from punishment may be violated in order to serve general interests marginally at best – if such a right may ever be violated. There is no symmetry of rights to punishment against offenders and rights of the innocent to be left alone.

What rights and/or interests may back punishment at all? No discussion has so far brought to light any really plausible justification of punishment as infliction of pain. What public interests are really served by such punishment? Even highly sophisticated combinations of retributive and preventive considerations trying to answer this question come in for sound criticism. Existing criminal

6   See, *e.g.* H.J.R. Kaptein, 'Against the pain of punishment: on penal servitude and procedural justice for all' in H.J.R. Kaptein and M. Malsch (eds.), *Crime, Victims and Justice: Essays on Principles and Practice* (Aldershot: Ashgate Publishing Limited, 2004), pp. 80–111.

institutions may be reformed of course, but still this problem of delegitimation remains.

Thus regarded, criminal law, criminal institutions and state punishment may have no more than an impressive air of legal ratio- nality, lacking any real foundation in the end. They probably can- not be done away with within any foreseeable time but still their delegitimation may lead to abstinence in the practice of criminal law whenever feasible. Or – to summarise – better leave the pos- sibly innocent alone than serve any unclear goal of punishment as infliction of pain. This problem of balancing is not limited to issues of insufficient evidence and proof of course.

Note that the same kind of reasoning justifies exclusion of improperly obtained evidence. Offenders may go free if the pub- lic interest is still better served by sanctioning police and public prosecution misconduct violating defendants' rights, even if the evidence concerned is empirically completely conclusive.

4.4 Victims of crime may not agree

However, it would seem then that such theorising is totally out of tune with the reasonable expectations of victims of crime. Victims of crime may be completely sure of the facts of their ordeal, imply- ing full criminal liability of the wrongdoers concerned. They may be right, even in cases of doubtful evidence and proof in the end, that is, from any court's standpoint. This may lead to a rather dif- ferent outcome of balancing: in cases of doubtful evidence, there is the small change of punishing the innocent versus the correspond- ingly high likelihood of leaving victims in the cold. This is no longer balancing rights of the innocent to go free against marginal general interests, but balancing rights of potential offenders versus victims' rights. Outcomes of this may be less clear.

Again, this may not be statistically significant. Even in the 10 per cent category not all kinds of crime concerned relate to specific victims. Nevertheless, individual cases bring to light tragedies of victims of crime left out in the cold as a consequence of defendants' acquittal on the basis of insufficient evidence. Thus victims of crime may come to believe that they are guilty themselves, as responsibil- ity and liability for their plight is not officially transferred to where it belongs. For many victims this guilt issue is of overwhelming importance, not least because they cannot simply 'do away with guilt'. If this guilt is not transferred to offenders, victims are stuck with it. This forceful psychic mechanism may lead to dire consequences for victims concerned.[7] Additionally, damages may not be paid to them, as a consequence of the acquittal of the offenders concerned. Generally, offenders' escaping sentencing and sanctioning harms victims once more.

One standard answer to this is to say that criminal law as public law was not designed to take care of victims in the first place. Accommodating victims of crime in criminal law and criminal proceedings creates only false hope. Both victims and general interests are to suffer if criminal law is further developed to ever more complex and inadequate patchworks of public law and 'private' victim–offender conflict resolution. So stick to criminal law as public law serving general interests only and try to take care of victims of crime by other and hopefully more adequate means. Or so it is contended.

But again: what justifies criminal law as public law serving general interests by inflicting pain to offenders (see Section 4.3 above)? Why not more radically try to reform criminal justice and see what may be done by it for victims of crime after all? As explained elsewhere, reinterpretation of retribution as reparation may be the key idea here.[8] Making offenders pay for what they did wrong may be rather more fruitful in so many respects than just making them suffer for no clear purposes.[9] Some of this is already practised of course, but generally on a small scale in legal and social environments rather hostile to the idea in general. Still retribution as reparation, both in material and in procedural aspects, may lead the way out of the predicament of current criminal justice, its huge costs and rather unclear rewards.

This is all very well but no solution at all for problems of insufficient evidence and proof, it may be retorted. Worse, retribution as

---

7   On this see, *e.g.*, several chapters in Kaptein and Malsch (eds.), *Crime, Victims and Justice.*

8   H.J.R. Kaptein, 'Against the pain of punishment: on penal servitude and procedural justice for all'.

9   C.B. Beccaria, *Dei delitti e delle pene* (Livorno, 1764 [1766]) also in R. Bellamy (ed.), *On Crimes and Punishments and Other Writings* (Cambridge University Press, 1995).

reparation is not just reparation to harm done to public interests, but may relate to harm done to individual victims of crime as well. So victim issues are back in the foreground again, including vexing problems of guilt transference. This only aggravates problems with standards of evidence and consequences of them in terms of *in dubio abstine*. Leaving all doubtful cases alone would really harm all victims concerned, then. Again, even if such cases may be rare, too much real and really undeserved victims' suffering may be the result.

From victims' standpoints, exclusion of improperly obtained but still conclusive evidence is one more way to rob them of their dues. Offenders may be definitely guilty but still escape sentencing as a consequence of official misconduct in collection of evidence against them. Indeed, a generally better solution of the problem of improperly obtained evidence may be sanctioning officials concerned and compensating offenders for harm done, so as to still make way for possibly conclusive evidence as a basis for conviction. (Criminal proceedings in Scandinavia may do rather better in this respect than criminal proceedings elsewhere.)

4.5   May 'civilisation' of evidence law solve the problem?

How does one get out of this '10 per cent predicament', leaving too many real victims of crime in the cold of undeserved acquittal? Hitherto it was taken for granted indeed that about 10 per cent of the facts of charges do not lend themselves to proof beyond any reasonable doubt. One basic presupposition of this is the existence of historical facts 'out there', independent of human perception. Otherwise it would make no sense to put it that something may have happened or may not have happened and that this cannot be established for sure on the basis of evidence available. Uncertainty necessarily relates to uncertainty about something, on which any probability statements may make sense then. Thus it makes sense to conjecture whether Jim killed Mary in Bergen sometime last year, whereas it would be senseless to assign any probability to Mary being a witch because she did not drown after being thrown in the swimming pool.

This of course is one of the mainstays of Benthamite thinking about evidence: The field of evidence is no other than the field of knowledge.[10]

Alternatively, there is something like a real past to be known in principle, at least in so far as relevant for criminal evidence. Human endeavours to establish such pasts may not always be successful, but at least ought to be hindered by legal formalities as little as possible. Torture in order to obtain confessions should be prohibited, other rules ought to set time limits to fact-finding procedures but that's more or less about it.[11]

Not just radical criticism of objective historical reality like presentism (as briefly discussed in Section 4.2) may undermine this. So many ontologies purport to demonstrate that there is no such thing as objective reality, past, present or future. Sceptical epistemologies echo this, in denying objective knowledge. Less radical views limit spheres of objective knowledge to the world of hard science, remote from human realities of criminal justice.[12]

Perspectivisms loom large here of course: knowledge of realities is taken to be subjective conception of realities as perceived from specific standpoints at best. Please note that even the staunchest of objectivists would not deny perspectivism in the psychological sense that subjective standpoints may distort reality. But this is rather different from ontological and/or epistemological perspectivism denying objective reality and/or objective knowledge. Psychological perspectivism on the other hand presupposes objectivity, or there would be no meaningful distortion in subjective standpoints. In fact any distinction of subjective versus objective does not make sense in really sceptical conceptions of knowledge and the world.

10 As summarised in Chapter 1, Part 1 of J. Bentham, 'An Introductory View of the Rationale of Evidence: For the Use of Non-Lawyers as well as Lawyers'[1812], in J. Bowring and J. Mill (eds.), *The Works of Jeremy Bentham*, Vol. 6 (Edinburgh: William Tait, 1843).

11 J. Bentham, *ibid.*, (1812) in Bowring and Mill (eds.) *The Works of Jeremy Bentham*, Vol. 6; 'Rationale of Judicial Evidence, Specially Applied to English Practice', From the manuscripts of Jeremy Bentham,... in five volumes, (ed.) J.S. Mill (London: Hunt and Clarke, 1827), (also in Bowring and Mill (eds.), *ibid.*) See W. Twining, *Theories of Evidence: Bentham and Wigmore* (London: Weidenfeld and Nicolson, 1985) for a slightly one-sided but still adequate introduction to these great and sometimes undeservedly forgotten works.

12 See Kaptein, Prakken and Verheij (eds.), *Legal Evidence and Proof* for criticism in so far as is relevant to criminal evidence and proof.

In fact these two different perspectivisms may lead to the same negative conclusion concerning any evidence based on objectively established historical facts. If such evidence is unattainable, be it for theoretical or just for practical reasons only, then any distinction between certain and uncertain evidence loses sense. Nothing much more than bits and pieces of evidence interpreted in terms of different stories from different perspectives remains, then. Or, the will-o'-the-wisp thing again ... (see Section 4.2 above).

Such doubts may lead to a conception of evidence and evidence law completely different from any conception referring to historical reality as the ultimate evidential basis. According to proceduralism (to give it a more or less adequate name) proof is not so much an issue of establishment of past realities on the basis of present evidence, with the help of general laws and logic, but of courts' conclusions drawn from different stories told by the parties concerned, according to fair rules of evidence law. Then proof is not a matter of science – as Bentham would have it – but of convincing a court that one story is more plausible than the other and thus ought to furnish the factual basis of the case. In such fashion, stories may still be useful for, or even constitutive of, legal evidence and proof (see Section 4.2 for earlier criticism of stories in contexts of legal proof as based on observation, general laws and logic). Put differently again: legal proof is fundamentally different from archeological and historical proof, then. This of course is part of at least civil evidence law in common law jurisdictions and elsewhere, historically based on ancient doubts about the establishment of past realities 'as they really were' (see Brundage on interesting backgrounds of this, dating back to the Middle Ages at least).[13]

May this lead victims of crime out of the 10 per cent predicament? They may be convinced that criminal conflict resolution ought not to be any frustratingly senseless search for hard historical facts 'as they were', but ought to come down to comparing stories of, and discussion between, parties concerned in order to reach a reasonable conclusion ending the conflict. Thus stories no longer play negative roles remote from the facts of the case (as suggested in Section 4.2), but are in fact the very starting point of a reasoned

---

13   J.A. Brundage, *The Medieval Origins of the Legal Profession: Canonists, Civilians and Courts* (University of Chicago Press, 2008).

procedure leading to an acceptable outcome of the conflict. Then even in the 10 per cent doubtful cases no more issues of criminal defendants wrongly going free at the expense of their victims remain. That is, if any 90 per cent/10 per cent distinction makes sense in proceduralism, denying the relevance of objective facts as possible bases for probability judgements as well.

In fact such conflict resolution constituting the facts of the case as a result of fair hearing and further procedure seems in line with important procedural aspects of restorative justice. Everybody concerned may have a say, according to the rules. Establishment of evidence is no longer taken away from the parties, in a vain search for any absolute truth of the matter by some higher body. So justice may be done, leading to end results more or less acceptable to benevolent participants. Not all convicted criminal defendants may agree, but then not all conflicts may always be solved to everybody's satisfaction.

Against this it is not a good argument in principle to state that outcomes of proceduralism in the actual practice of civil and criminal evidence law are largely determined by false rhetoric, unequal resources of the parties concerned and other factors distorting its principles. Other problems encountered in practice, however, may bring to light serious defects in the very idea of proceduralism in matters of evidence and proof. Firstly, there is the presumption of innocence protecting criminal defendants. In itself this is a norm prescribing officials and others to – possibly counterfactually – treat citizens, suspects and criminal defendants as if they were innocent, until there is a final authoritative decision implying otherwise. Thus (and this against popular legal conviction) criminal defendants' rights not to contribute to their conviction is not at all a direct consequence of the presumption of innocence. Still there are good reasons of course for defendants' rights to remain silent, apart from minor technical exceptions in several jurisdictions.[14]

Such defendants' silence however may have dire consequences, at least according to proceduralism. One basic tenet of proceduralist evidence law is that any more or less plausible standpoint put forward by one side according to the rules that is not contradicted

---

14   See, however, European Court of Human Rights, 'Salabiaku' (7.10.1988), A 141, NJ, 1991, 351., for more serious exceptions.

by the other side is not just legally relevant but may be the basis for the final conclusion. Thus a defendant enjoying his right to remain silent may end up in jail for the wrong reasons. Or, here the fallacy of argumentation *ad ignorantiam* may be committed: absence of argumentation for a standpoint does not imply denial of the same standpoint.

Also, not all victims of crime live to tell their stories in court. Surviving victims such as family members may not always be able to offer first-hand evidence of the crime concerned. Even less symmetry, one mainstay of proceduralism, may be the result.

More generally it may be put against proceduralism that its application may lead to results at odds with historical reality. Witnesses may be mistaken, or *mala fide*, material evidence seemingly backing some stories and contradicting others may be misinterpreted, etc.

This is a *petitio principii*, however, as the idea of proceduralism is based among other things on the theoretical or practical absence of any objective historical reality. Or, again: legal evidence and proof are categorically different from archeological and historical evidence and proof. If this holds good, even argumentation *ad ignorantiam* is not really fallacious according to proceduralism, as any such fallacy presupposes some or other truth independent of any given argumentation.

Still this has at least an air of the absurd, as brought out probably unintentionally by US Supreme Court Associate Justice Scalia: 'Mere factual innocence is no reason not to carry out a death sentence properly reached.'[15]

Not just everything may be true in one perspective only, or subjective, or relative, or whatever. In fact proceduralism reduces the establishment of evidence and proof to nothing more than processes of complex counteracting rhetorical and other forces leading to some or other end result without any reference to any non-procedural criterion. Pure procedural justice is to establish the facts of the case, according to such proceduralism. Within its bounds, a meta-conflict is fought out in order to end the original conflict. What in the end is the difference between this and pre-medieval

---

15 Supreme Court of the United States of America, *Herrera v. Collins* [506 US 390] (1993), Opinion of Associate Justice Antonin Scalia.

'legal' fights to determine who is right? Everything worthwhile seems to disappear in the flow of things, without any real reference points. This and more is well stated by Frankfurt:

> our recognition and our understanding of our own identity arises out of, and depends integrally on, our appreciation of a reality that is definitively independent of ourselves. In other words, it arises out of and depends on our recognition that there are facts and truths over which we cannot hope to exercise direct or immediate control. If there were no such facts or truths, if the world invariably and unresistingly became whatever we might like or wish it to be, we would be unable to distinguish ourselves from what is other than ourselves and we would have no sense of what in particular we ourselves are. It is only through our recognition of a world of stubbornly independent reality, fact, and truth that we come both to recognise ourselves as beings distinct from others and to articulate the specific nature of our own identities.
>
> How, then, can we fail to take the importance of factuality and of reality seriously? How can we fail to care about truth?
>
> We cannot.[16]

Let this solemnly end any proceduralism, not just in establishment of such important matters as facts of charges. Please note that evidential proceduralism relating to facts is different from probably more plausible pure procedural justice relating to norms and values.[17] Furthermore, stark contrasts drawn here between historical proof and proceduralist proof intentionally overlook all kinds of mixtures of them in practice, both in civil and in criminal procedure. All the worse for such legal practice, one would say. The one and only end to be served by evidence law is and remains: bringing to light what happened in so far as legally relevant. Procedures are to be instrumental to that purpose, not constitutive of any evidence and proof themselves.

So 'civilisation' of criminal evidence law on behalf of victims is not a good idea at all. A still worse idea would be to relegate

---

16   H.G. Frankfurt, *On Truth* (New York: Alfred A. Knopf, 2006), pp. 100f.

17   Rawls, *A Theory of Justice* [1971] (Cambridge, M A: Belknap Press of Harvard University Press, 1999) and S. Hampshire, *Justice is Conflict* (Princeton University Press, 2000).

victims of crime to civil law and civil procedure completely. Even if civil evidence law may have evolved away from proceduralism in the search for more historical truth in some jurisdictions, too many victims of crime cannot get their rightful dues by such civil means. The problems are probably too well known to warrant any lengthy discussion: civil procedure is expensive, time-consuming, and leading to outcomes more dependent on the parties' legal and other resources than on the material merits of the cases concerned, not just as a consequence of the proceduralist establishment of evidence.

Damages are paid by insurance money and not by defendants themselves, in more than a few cases. This is not necessarily a good thing for victims, as such exoneration may not satisfy their interests in the identification of real offenders and their liabilities. Alternatively, payment by insurance money seems to imply that the offenders concerned were not really responsible and thus do not need to pay. One extreme example of this is to be found in a Supreme Court adjudication in the Netherlands in 1998:[18] a man convicted of grievous bodily harm with lasting consequences leading to serious disabilities was exonerated in civil court. It was judged that his *mens rea* was not directed toward any harmful consequences, but simply for 'the fun of it'. Strangely counterfactual as this may seem, its implicit motivation probably was to get around insurance law obstacles excluding payment in cases of any criminal intent. Thus the victim got his (insurance) money, while being told that the offender was not responsible for what he did after all.

Another strange development in civil adjudication however may lead the way to an elegant and effective solution of the 90 per cent/10 per cent issue – with which the whole discussion here started of course. Thus the same Supreme Court decided (in 2006) that an asbestos processing enterprise had to pay 60 per cent of the damages to a former employee's widow, because no acceptable certainty could be reached about the contribution of other causes to relevant damage, such as smoking tobacco. Why not apply this brilliant invention – called proportional liability and not just found in the Netherlands – in criminal proceedings as well? Then doubtful cases in the 10 per cent category may be decided on the basis of

---

18   Supreme Court of the Netherlands, 'AGEON II' (6 November 1998), *NJ* 1999, 220.

the relevant probabilities, such as: there is still a 90 per cent chance the defendant did it, so he receives 90 per cent of the sentence.

The blatant absurdity of this category error is not just a consequence of the inapplicability of any quantitative probabilities to individual human conduct of course. In civil law some justification for such opportunistic reasoning may be found in the implicit moral (?) principle that victims should get at least some insurance money even in cases of doubtful tort. (If all this is too casuistic on the shortcomings of tort law please consult Atiyah.[19]) – Which is not to deny that some victims of crime do profit from (threats of) civil procedure leading to payment of damages.

4.6 One way out of the predicament: State liability

So not much progress has been made yet. No conception of evidence and proof investigated up to now offers a good solution. There may better conceptions and practices of evidence and proof of course, though the aim of determining legally relevant historical facts probably remains the main issue of any theory and practice of evidence law. So the 10 per cent or thereabout issue survived it all, with a vengeance, tort law offering no way out either, not even in determining damages by evidential probabilities.

Some consolation, however, for victims of crime left out in the cold as a consequence of insufficient evidence and proof against offenders having harmed them may be found by 'halving' the evidence and proof issue. Why not reduce the problem to determining victims' harm, at least in cases of doubtful evidence against possibly innocent defendants? In many cases, evidence and proof of victims' wrongful harm is more readily available than evidence against the offenders concerned. One reason for this of course is the greater willingness of victims to co-operate in the establishment of evidence concerning their plight, as compared with offenders being generally unwilling to concede their criminal liabilities.

What are victims to gain by this? Their victimhood established, they still get no satisfaction at all by identification of the really guilty among the 10 per cent category, who simply go free

19 P.S. Atiyah, *The Damages Lottery*, (Oxford: Hart Publishing, 1997).

– unless it makes sense to identify another responsible body: the state. States and specific public administration bodies are held to be responsible and liable for just about everything, from public housing, road safety, education, defence and so many more things in the ever-expanding catalogue of citizens' expectations of 'the nanny state' expected to care for everything. Not just in this light – or darkness – is it strange that public responsibility for citizens' freedom from crime is generally recognised, but no corresponding liability at all. So why not make the state liable for crime? This liability may be completely transferred to offenders against whom conclusive evidence and proof is established. In doubtful cases, however, defendants may go free, while the state assumes full liability instead.

Thus the state may be 'punished' at least in symbolic fashion by having to accept full liability for 'offenderless' crimes, by official court rulings. One more advantage may be the loosening of negative emotional bonds between victims and offenders, by interposing the state. Unorthodox as this may seem, it may well be a way out of the 10 per cent predicament.

Indeed such liability by the state for crime goes rather further than just state compensation for victims of crime. Liability by the state for crime presupposes some or other offence and it may not be completely clear what kind of crime is committed by the state in not preventing victimisation. This may come down to something like the state's general duty or obligation to protect citizens by preventing undue violence. Violation of this may be regarded as a crime, then – leaving out of account classical objections according to which states by definition cannot commit crimes. This is factually impossible anyway, though some good work may still be done here.

So why not limit the scheme to compensation payments? But then just paying off victims may not do. Victims do need more than money and/or other kinds of redress, they need to know they are not liable for their plights themselves. Indeed courts' ceremonial and authoritative determination of criminal liability and its consequences in terms of victims' compensation remains of great importance. It may still console some victims, by transferring guilt away from them, however anonymously. This may be one important function of liability by the state for crime, however symbolic or even metaphorical, though it is clear enough that some more thought and action may be needed before anything like this is to be realised.

Still such state liability may come down to at least some kind of solution not just in cases of inconclusive evidence against criminal defendants. So many other offenders are not even identified at all. Their victims are not to be left out in the cold either. It may even do good to all victims of crime – though of course such state liability does not imply letting all suspects, defendants and offenders go free.

Advantages may include lower cost and generally greater efficiency in handling crime victim cases. Parallels may here be drawn with the New Zealand Accident Compensation System (as revised in 2001), and with state compensation for victims of crime in Norway (as further reformed by legislation in 2001 as well), among others, though liability by the state for crime goes rather further of course.

There may be more principled justification for it as well. If the state is reasonably expected to protect citizens against criminal harm, then this duty indeed implies corresponding liability. This liability implies not just going after criminal suspects, but also minimising the consequences of crime. (On the legal symmetries of avoiding and repairing wrongful harm see also Kaptein.[20]) One important way to do this is to compensate victims of crime fully if no offenders can be conclusively identified. Payment of such damages may both express state liability and materially comfort victims of crime. This may also be a way out of victims' predicaments as consequences of offenders' inability to realise compensation themselves.

In fact, if criminal justice is to be really public law, such state care for victims is an essential part of it.[21]

Disadvantages may include state payment to 'false victims'. But

---

20 H.J.R. Kaptein, 'Virtues of Truth in Forbearing Wrongs: Client Confidentiality Qualified by Legal Symmetry of Past and Future Harm' in A. Amaya and H.L. Ho (eds.), *Law, Virtue and Justice* (Oxford: Hart Publishing, 2011).

21 For a more fundamental justification of state liability for crime, and also in terms of fellow citizens' responsibility for each other to be organised by the state as a basis of criminal law and punishment to be reformed in terms of retribution as reparation, see Kaptein and Malsch (eds.), *Crime, Victims and Justice* (Aldershot: Ashgate Publishing, 2004).

then this is no longer done at the cost of innocent criminal defendants. Additionally, compensation may still be offered in doubtful cases of victimhood, so as to err on the safe side, again not wrongfully harming the innocent. Thus problems of proof or the absence of it are rather less pressing here.

4.7 Agenda

State liability for crime in the interest of victims may not be realised within any foreseeable future, however rational it may be. This of course is the case with other reforming proposals of the practice of criminal law, or for that matter of human life in general. So what could be done in the meantime, not just to alleviate the problem of victims left out in the cold through acquittal as a consequence of insufficient evidence and proof? Suggestions offered here may be rather self-evident. Still summing them up (non-exhaustively of course) may not be completely useless, if only because actual practice does not always live up to such rather plain commonsense.

Firstly, and sometimes forgotten in unduly punitive times, there is and remains the overriding need to prevent crime in the first place, if possible somehow by more humane means than threats of punishment as infliction of pain. Much work is still to be done here – as explained before so many times. Not only the state has a role to play here. In fact, everybody however informally concerned with potentially criminal fellow human beings is to do his or her best to prevent victimisation and seriously unlawful behaviour in general. Potential victims themselves are to take due care so as not to be wrongfully harmed in the first place.

Secondly, if crime is committed after all, at the expense of victims, try to handle the consequences of it without having recourse to criminal proceedings. Thus – and again self-evident but insufficiently realised – mediation and other forms of informal conflict resolution may be rather more effective than any formal sanctioning, both for victims and for offenders, still apart from the preventive effects to be expected from offenders' confrontation with consequences of their misconduct. Such informal options may even persuade offenders to confess informally and to co-operate in further fact-finding, given the less attractive alternatives in terms of criminal proceedings and punishment. Thus a small part of the 10 per cent problem may be solved, sometimes without explicit recourse to any criminal proceedings.

Thirdly, police and public prosecutors' attention to crime ought to be directed to protecting potential victims and serving real victims in the first place. Both surveillance and investigation policies are to take this priority into account. Remember that police and/or public prosecutors' investigation leading to suspects related to specific victims does not necessarily lead to formal criminal proceedings. Alternative dispute resolution may even be initiated by the police and/or public prosecutors' offices.

Fourthly, if criminal proceedings are really unavoidable, heed the requirements of proportionality and subsidiarity in the first place. Victims' and others' rights and interests are not served by legal overkill anyway. This holds good not just for specific reactions to individual crime, but for criminal law in general as well. Otherwise, do not criminalise any conduct unless there is an overriding need to do so. As Beccaria stated time and again:[22] every new criminal law creates new crime. This is more than just a tautology of course. Saddening developments worldwide tell another story, in the 'development' of juvenile criminal law and the criminalisation of presumably undesirable conduct better channelled in other ways. All this wrongly diverts resources away from really serious crime and its victims as well.

Fifth, criminal conviction ought to be based on proof beyond reasonable doubt based on relevant historical facts. Victims of crime are not at all served by convictions in doubtful cases. State liability is a much better solution for lack of sufficient evidence and proof (Section 4.6). Anyway, much can be done in order to improve criminal fact-finding. Forensic science and evidence may be further perfected, officials concerned may be still better educated in the handling of, and argumentation concerning, the evidence, testimonial and otherwise. Thus not only false acquittals harming victims but also false convictions may be further avoided. Do away with any proceduralism, not just in criminal evidence law.

Sixth, do remember that victims are not served by ever harsher punishments. Punitive tendencies are fostered by so-called solidar-

22   Beccaria, *Dei delitti e delle pene.*

ity with victims of crime, whereas victims themselves are interested in offenders' official conviction and the attendant shifting-away of guilt from victims to offenders in the first place.

Seventh, financial and other kinds of compensation and reparation for victims of crime ought to be furthered by all means, not just by making offenders pay. Sometimes even civil procedures may do some good here indeed. Again, state liability and its compensatory consequences would be a more adequate solution.

Eighth, beware of dangers of excessive victimisation as a consequence of wrongful harm. This may be a good thing to contemplate even for victims themselves. Not everybody will be able to take a stoic position, such as: things happened as they happened, personal liberty is not to be found in choice in the first place, but in freedom in reaction to fate, offenders were not really free themselves either, what is the sense of punishment against such offenders in a deterministic world anyway? etc. Still, such a philosophy of life may make sense at times. It may be an important part of regaining personal autonomy, at least in the sense of being the master of one's own world again.

Ninth, and again not limited to victims harmed by offenders' acquittal on the basis of insufficient evidence and proof, care for victims of crime by professionals and non-professionals in the non-legal world – or the real world some would say – may be at least as important as any legal remedies for victims of crime. Even psychologists and others lending attentive ears may mean more to victims of crime than legal officials and (other) lawyers, let alone academic legal writers on restorative justice.

Tenth,... and so on, and so on. Let's keep up the good work. Many thanks to Jørn Jacobsen, Elisa van Ee and Tristan Heringa, for their fruitful comments and corrections at this intermediate stage.

References

Amaya, A., and Ho, H.L., (eds.), *Law, Virtue and Justice* (Oxford: Hart Publishing, 2011).

Atiyah, P.S., *The Damages Lottery* (Oxford: Hart Publishing, 1997).

Beccaria, C.B., *Dei delitti e delle pene* (Livorno, 1764 [1766]) also in R. Bellamy (ed.), *On Crimes and Punishments and Other Writings* (Cambridge University Press, 1995).

Bentham, J., *An Introductory View of the Rationale of Evidence: For the Use of Non-Lawyers as well as Lawyers* [1812], in J. Bowring and J. Mill (eds.), *The Works of Jeremy Bentham*, Vol. 6 (Edinburgh: William Tait, 1843).

Rationale of Judicial Evidence, Specially Applied to English Practice, From the manuscripts of Jeremy Bentham,... In five volumes, (ed.) J.S. Mill (London: Hunt and Clarke, 1827) (also in Bowring and Mill (eds.), *The Works of Jeremy Bentham*).

Brundage, J.A., *The Medieval Origins of the Legal Profession: Canonists, Civilians and Courts* (University of Chicago Press, 2008).

Derksen, T., and Meijsing, M., 'The Fabrication of Facts: The Lure of the Incredible Coincidence' in H.J.R. Kaptein, H. Prakken and B. Verheij, (eds.), *Legal Evidence and Proof* (as below).

European Court of Human Rights, 'Salabiaku' (7.10.1988), A 141, *NJ*, 1991, 351.

Frankfurt, H.G., *On Truth* (New York: Alfred A. Knopf, 2006).

Hampshire, S., *Justice is Conflict* (Princeton University Press, 2000).

Johnstone, G., and Van Ness, D.W., *Handbook of Restorative Justice* (Cullompton, Devon, UK: Willan Publishing, 2006).

Kaptein, H.J.R., 'Against the Pain of Punishment: On Penal Servitude and Procedural Justice for All' in H.J.R. Kaptein and M. Malsch (eds.), *Crime, Victims and Justice* (as below), pp. 80–111.

'Rigid Anarchic Principles of Proof: Anomist Panaceas Against Legal Pathologies of Proceduralism' in H.J.R. Kaptein, H. Prakken and B. Verheij, (eds.), *Legal Evidence and Proof* (as below), pp. 195–221.

'Virtues of Truth in Forbearing Wrongs: Client Confidentiality Qualified by Legal Symmetry of Past and Future Harm' in A. Amaya and H.L. Ho, (eds.), *Law, Virtue and Justice* (as above).

Kaptein, H.J.R., and Malsch, M., (eds.), *Crime, Victims and Justice: Essays on Principles and Practice* (Aldershot: Ashgate Publishing, 2004)

Kaptein, H.J.R., Prakken H., and Verheij, B., (eds.), *Legal Evidence and Proof: Statistics, Stories, Logic* (Farnham and Burlington: Ashgate Publishing, 2009).

Malsch, M., and Nijboer, J.F., (eds.), *Complex Cases: Perspectives on the Netherlands Criminal Justice System* (Amsterdam: Thela Thesis, 1999).

Netherlands, Supreme Court of the, 'AEGON II' (6.11.1998), *NJ* 1999, 220.

Karamus v. Nefalit (31.01.2006), *RvdW* 2006, 328.

New Zealand, Parliament of, *Injury Prevention, Rehabilitation, and*

Compensation Act, Public Act 2001 No. 49, Date of assent: 19 September 2001.

Norway, Kingdom of, ('Act on compensation for victims of violent crimes') (1 July 2001).

Rawls, J., *A Theory of Justice* [1971], (Cambridge, MA: Belknap Press of Harvard University Press, 1999).

Schafer, S., *Compensation and Restitution to Victims of Crime* [1960] (Montclair, NJ: Patterson Smith, 1970).

Twining, W., *Theories of Evidence: Bentham and Wigmore* (London: Weidenfeld and Nicolson, 1985)

United States of America, Supreme Court of the, *Herrera* v. *Collins* [506 US 390] (1993), Opinion of Associate Justice Antonin Scalia.

Wagenaar, W.A., van Koppen, P.J., and Crombag, H.F.M., *Anchored Narratives: The Psychology of Criminal Evidence* (Hemel Hempstead, Hertfordshire, UK: Harvester Wheatsheaf, and New York: St. Martin's Press, 1993.)

5. Restorative justice in the Norwegian juvenile justice system

INGUN FORNES[1]

5.1 Introduction

Since the use of restorative justice programmes was introduced in Norway at the beginning of the 1980s, there has been a significant increase in the use of such programmes. Restorative justice is used both as an alternative and a supplement to the traditional criminal justice system. Most of the programmes and measures based on the principles of restorative justice in Norway are – in some way – attached to the mediation boards. The well-known article by Nils Christie, 'Conflicts as property',[2] evidently inspired the introduction of the mediation boards in Norway.

At the start of the introduction of restorative justice in Norway, such programmes were reserved for juvenile offenders.[3] Today, restorative justice can be used both in criminal and civil cases, and there are no age limits restricting which cases can be referred

---

1   The author would especially like to thank post doc. Jørn R. T. Jacobsen and post doc. Linda Gröning for commenting on this chapter several times. The author also would like to thank senor lecturer Hendrik Kaptein for commenting on a late version of the chapter. Since this chapter was written the changes in the law proposed in the White Paper NOU 2008:15 and discussed in section 5.5 has been passed. Some changes are made to the original proposition. As the discussion in section 5.5 still might be of interest it is kept here.

2   N. Christie, 'Conflicts as Property', *The British Journal of Criminology*, 17 (1), 1977, pp. 1–15.

3   The first mediation board ('Konfliktrådet i Lier, et forsøk på alternative konfliktløsing') was a part of the project 'Alternativ til fengsling av ungdom' (Alternatives to imprisonment of juveniles). NOU 1985: 3 *Tiltak for ungdom med atferdsvansker*, pp. 96–97 and NOU 2008: 15 *Barn og straff – utviklingsstøtte og kontroll*, p. 18.

to the mediation boards. Even though there are no age limits, juvenile offenders are still the largest group of defendants in the mediation boards. Restorative justice programmes are often seen as a particularly well-suited response where the offender is under age. Both the Norwegian Ministry of Justice and Police and the Norwegian Director-General of Public Prosecution emphasise that they want restorative justice to be used more often in the criminal justice system and that such programmes are particularly well suited where the offender is young. The Ministry of Justice and Police has declared that, in offences where the offence is confessed and a victim is identified, a dialogue with restoration and reconciliation as the primary goal shall always be set up if possible. Such an approach can be of interest at all levels and at all times after the crime has been committed – before, during and after the sentence is served.[4] The Director-General of Public Prosecution has in his annual directive to the police since 2003 emphasised every year that the use of referrals to the mediation boards should be increased. Furthermore, he has several times emphasised in particular the wish for more referrals to the mediation boards where the offender is under age.[5]

In Section 5.3 I shall point out how restorative justice is understood in Norway, *i.e.* how these principles seem to be understood in practical life. I shall also show that there is a lack of theoretical discussion on how restorative justice should be understood in Norwegian jurisprudence. In Section 5.4 I shall, to some extent, make a starting point for such a theoretical discussion by outlining the different stages of the criminal proceedings where restorative justice is used given that the offender was under 18 years of age at the time of the crime. I shall also discuss the particular advantages and challenges one faces when using restorative justice at different stages of the criminal proceedings. I shall focus on juvenile offenders, but the similarity in the treatment of juvenile and adult offenders in Norwegian criminal law makes this discussion also relevant where the offender is an adult. In some areas there are no differences either in the approach to minor and adult offenders or in the advantages and challenges one

---

4   St.meld. 37 (2007–2008) *Straff som virker* ['Punishment That Works'] – *mindre kriminalitet – tryggere samfunn (Kriminalomsorgsmelding)*, p. 164.
5   Most recently in Riksadvokatens rundskriv: *Mål og prioriteringer for straffesaksbehandlingen i politiet* – 2010.

faces using restorative justice arrangements at the different stages of criminal proceedings. I shall not exclude these areas from the text, but shall point out where one cannot find such differences, as these areas are an important part of the discussion as well.

In one of the stages presented (Section 5.5), I shall discuss a new penal response reserved for juvenile offenders and based on the principles of restorative justice (youth conference), proposed in the white paper NOU 2008: 15.[6] The Norwegian Parliament has at this point not yet decided on whether this response should become a part of the Norwegian criminal justice system. The proposition will be further discussed in Section 5.5 where I discuss this development and its possible future. In this section I shall show how the proposed response of a youth conference seems to become a melting-pot of different responses towards juvenile offenders – a feature that seems to have both positive and negative aspects.

First of all, however, it is necessary briefly to present the 'Norwegian juvenile justice system'. This will be done in Section 5.2.

5.2 'The Norwegian juvenile justice system'

Properly speaking there is no 'Norwegian juvenile justice system': there is not a particular system reserved for juvenile offenders in Norway, and a corresponding term is actually not used in Norwegian. There are no special laws regulating juvenile delinquency and there are no juvenile courts. Juvenile, and minor, offenders are essentially treated in the same manner as adult offenders.

In accordance with § 46 of the Penal Code,[7] in Norway juvenile offenders are persons who have turned 15, but not yet turned 18, years of age at the time of the crime, cf. § 1 section 2 the Guardianship Act.[8] There are no special provisions concerning young offenders who have already turned 18 at the time of the crime. When a person

---

6   NOU 2008: 15 *Barn og straff – utviklingsstøtte og kontroll.*

7   Almindelig borgerlig Straffelov 22. mai 1902 nr. 10 (Straffeloven). The General Civil Penal Code 22 May 1902 No. 10 (The Penal Code).

8   Lov 22. april 1927 nr. 3 om vergemål for umyndige (vergemålsloven). Act of 22 April 1927 No. 3 relating to guardianship for persons who are legally incapable (The Guardianship Act).

turns 18, he or she is considered to be an adult and thus treated as an adult in the criminal justice system. His or her age can, however, be taken into account in, for instance, sentencing, and in some regards even function as an excuse and as a reason for refraining from punishment, *cf.* §§ 196 of the Penal Code.

Juvenile offenders are bound by the same penalty provisions as adults. Furthermore, there are no special penal sanctions reserved for juvenile offenders, nor are there, as mentioned, any youth courts in Norway. An indictment against a minor will always be tried in a normal court of law. The criminal proceedings where the accused person is under 18 years old are in general equivalent to the criminal proceedings where the accused person is an adult.

Even though a particular system reserved for juvenile offenders does not exist, there are a few – but important – provisions in the Norwegian Criminal Proceedings Act[9] and in the Penal Code framed to protect the special interests of persons charged, or offenders, who are minors. The Criminal Proceedings Act § 174, *cf.* § 184, states that a person under 18 years of age should not be remanded in custody unless it is especially necessary, and the Penal Code § 55 states that the penalty may be reduced below the minimum prescribed for the act and, when circumstances so indicate, to a milder form of penalty. In addition, the UN Convention on the Rights of the Child is incorporated into Norwegian law, *cf.* the Human Rights Act § 2.[10] Its articles concerning juvenile offenders will prevail if there is a conflict between domestic Norwegian law and the convention, *cf.* the Human Rights Act § 3. By incorporating this Convention into Norwegian law, the principle of the best interest of the child has been introduced into Norwegian criminal law as well. The principle is well known in Norwegian family and children law, but the application of this principle in criminal cases has been rather slow in developing. A possible reason for this is that the courts already consider the domestic criminal law to be in accordance with this principle.[11]

9   Lov 22. mai 1981 nr. 25 om rettergangen i straffesaker (straffeprosessloven). The Criminal Procedure Act 22 May 1981 No. 25.

10 Lov 21. mai 1999 nr. 30 om styrking av menneskerettighetenes stilling i norsk rett (menneskerettsloven). The Human Rights Act 21 May 1999 No. 30.

11 A recent judgment from the Norwegian Supreme Court (HR-2010-1849-A) might be the starting point of a more active application of this principle by

A special feature of the Norwegian juvenile justice system is the distinct role of the Child Welfare Service. The Child Welfare Service has different measures to hand, which can be used where a minor displays behavioural problems. One of these measures is to place a child into an institution without the child's or the parents' (or alternatively the legal guardian's) consent, when the child has committed serious or repeated crimes, *cf.* the Child Welfare Service Act § 4–24.[12] The Child Welfare Service is regulated in a separate code, the Child Welfare Act, and is not considered to be a part of the criminal justice system. On the contrary, it is often pointed out that the measures applied by the Child Welfare Service shall not be used as penal sanctions, but as rehabilitative measures used in the best interests of the child. These measures are imposed by an administrative decision.

As mentioned above there are no special penal sanctions reserved for juvenile offenders. Even though there are no special sanctions, some sanctions are used more often where the offender is under age. The best example of such a sanction is referral of the case to the mediation board, *cf.* the Criminal Proceedings Act § 71a. Furthermore, the lack of special codes regarding juvenile offenders does not necessarily imply that the government does not focus on this group of offenders. There has been an ongoing debate on the question of how to deal with juvenile delinquency since the end of the nineteenth century.[13] Different legal models to solve the problems of dealing with juvenile offenders have been tried during the last century.[14] The reluctance to create special laws regarding juvenile offenders, as we see it today, seems to be linked to the negative experiences from the era of rehabilitation. Since the end of this era there have been numerous experiments where one has tried to find responses especially suited to minors and in accordance with the current legal rules. Both local and governmental authorities have initiated these experiments, and many of them have been based on the principles of restorative justice.

---

the courts in criminal cases.

12 Lov 17. juli 1992 nr. 100 om barneverntjenester (barnevernloven). The Child Welfare Service Act 17 July 1992 No. 100.

13 *E.g.* F. Hagerup, *Forhandlinger ved Den Norske Kriminalistforenings første møte i oktober 1892*, (Kristiania: Aschehoug, 1895).

14 *E.g.* R. Hauge, *Straffens begrunnelser*, (Oslo: Universitetsforlaget, 1996).

5.3 How is 'restorative justice' understood in Norway?

There is no generally accepted definition of restorative justice, but it is fair to say that there is a common agreement that the ultimate object of restorative justice is to reconcile the victim, the offender and the community. In the further exploration of what restorative justice is one sees that different authors have different focuses. This is reflected in the different definitions proposed. Some definitions of restorative justice are process-based and some are outcome-based.[15] An often quoted process-based definition is Marshall's: 'Restorative justice is a process whereby all parties with a stake in a particular offence come together to resolve collectively how to deal with the aftermath of the offence and its implications for the future.'[16] Lode Walgrave uses an outcome-based definition: restorative justice is seen as 'an option on doing justice after the occurrence of a crime which gives priority to repair the harm that has been caused by the crime.'[17]

Even though the use of mediation is widespread in Norway, there are few theoretical discussions in Norwegian jurisprudence on restorative justice. In the discussion, restorative justice seems to be equated with the work of the mediation boards, which are the main supplier of restorative justice arrangements in Norway. The mediation boards have traditionally arranged victim–offender mediation, but lately some of the mediation boards have also started arranging group conferences. This restorative process also seems to be the main focus of reports and literature on restorative justice.

Norwegian criminal law offers the option of community service as a penal sanction and the courts may in criminal cases provide restitution to victims of crime as well. But none of these measures, often presented as restorative in international literature on restorative justice,[18] are traditionally considered as restorative measures

---

15 See K. Doolin, 'But What Does It Mean? Seeking Definitional Clarity in Restorative Justice', *The Journal of Criminal Law*, 2006–07, pp. 427–440.

16 T.F. Marshall, *Restorative Justice: an Overview*, (London: [British] Home Office, Research and Statistics Directorate, 1999) p. 5.

17 L. Walgrave, 'Restoration in Youth Justice', *Crime and Justice*, 31, 2004, p. 552.

18 *E.g.* M.S. Umbreit, 'Holding Juvenile Offenders Accountable: A Restorative Justice Perspective', *Juvenile and Family Court Journal*, 1995, pp. 31–42; L.

in Norway. An obvious reason for this is that these measures are neither the result of a restorative process nor, at least in the case of community service, do they have a particularly restorative outcome as it is practised today. The restitution to victims of crime might perhaps be seen as having an intended restorative outcome, but as the Norwegian Criminal Proceedings Act offered the option of providing such compensation to the victim in criminal cases many years before the restorative justice movement came into being, this restitution has as far as I know never been connected to the concept of restorative justice in Norway.[19]

An increased focus on what restorative justice is and how one can implement more restorative measures in the criminal justice system might perhaps also result in changes to the criminal proceedings and the framing of community service orders – increasing both the share of restorative process and restorative outcomes in the criminal justice system. However, changing a system that has developed for hundreds of years needs more than discussion of the possibilities existing in restorative justice – there is also need for a theoretical discussion, oriented towards the possibilities for a restorative justice reform in Norwegian criminal law, on the strengths and limitations of the current criminal justice system and the values that it represents. The criminal justice system plays an important role in the *Rechtsstaat* (rule of law)[20] and the fundamental principles of this legal order should at least be discussed, when radical changes to it are discussed. In this paper I shall address some of these questions, but the scope of the paper places a limitation on these discussions here.

Walgrave and H. Geudens, 'The Restorative Proportionality of Community Service for Juveniles', *European Journal of Crime, Criminal Law and Criminal Justice*, 1996, pp. 361–80.

19   The Norwegian Criminal Procedure Law of 1887 offered the option of this possibility in criminal cases.

20   See footnote 2, Chapter 1.

5.4 Restorative justice in Norwegian criminal law

5.4.1 *The starting point*

In Norway, victim–offender mediation has been used in cases where the offender is under age for almost thirty years. The first mediation board was established in 1981 as an experiment, and in 1992 the National Mediation Service Act came into force. Different authorities have emphasised that mediation should be available at all stages of the criminal justice system.[21] The European Forum for Victim–Offender Mediation and Restorative Justice has in its handbook 'Rebuilding community connections – mediation and restorative justice in Europe' outlined six stages where mediation can occur: (1) independently of the criminal justice system; (2) when referred by the police or prosecution at pre-court stage, or by the judge before the main hearing; (3) parallel to prosecution; (4) after conviction and before sentencing; (5) as part of and/or in addition to non-custodial sentence and (6) in prison, post-sentence or pre-release.[22] In this section I shall look into these different stages and examine to what extent restorative justice arrangements are used in the different stages of the Norwegian juvenile justice system. In addition I shall discuss some of the particular advantages and challenges of using restorative justice at these different stages. Where restorative justice is fully taking the place of criminal justice, it deserves some more reflections in particular. This will be done at the end of this section.

5.4.2 *Mediation and restorative justice occurring independently of the criminal justice system – stage (1)*

The relations between the criminal justice system and the mediation boards are to some extent codified in the Criminal Proceedings

---

21 *Cf.* Section 1. See also: The Committee of Ministers, Council of Europe: Recommendation No. R (*99*) 19 of the Committee of Ministers to Member States Concerning Mediation in Penal Matters, Appendix Section II 5, United Nations Economic and Social Council Resolution ECOSOC Resolution 2002/12 Section II 6.

22 Council of Europe Publishing, *Rebuilding Community Connections – Mediation and Restorative Justice*, written by Ivo Aertsen, Robert Mackay, Christa Pelikan, Martin Wright and Jolien Willemsens for the Council of Europe, (Strasbourg: 2004), p. 21.

Act and the National Mediation Service Act. Where an offence is committed and the perpetrator has passed the minimum age of responsibility, a case referred to the mediation board will in all essentials be treated as a criminal case. In most of these cases the offender's participation in a restorative justice arrangement will have an effect on the criminal case. Therefore it is not correct to consider these arrangements as occurring independently of the criminal justice system.

However, it is also possible to refer a case to the mediation board where a child below the age of 15 has committed an act that would have been punishable if it had been committed above the minimum age of criminal responsibility. These cases are treated as 'civil cases' and not criminal cases in the mediation boards. There is no formal or legal connection between the mediation and the criminal justice system in these cases. The case will not be prosecuted if the child does not consent to the referral or does not fulfil the agreement set out in the mediation – there is not a hidden treat as there will be in the criminal cases. Cases were the defender is age 12–14 were the second largest group of defendants in the mediation boards in 2007 and the third largest group of defendants in 2009.[23] In these cases the restorative justice arrangement occurs independently of the criminal justice system.

There are also some other restorative justice programmes existing independently of the criminal justice system. The Mediation on the Streets programmes, in which juveniles are trained in how to deal with conflicts, have been established in Oslo and Tromsø. A part of these projects is to step in where incidents happen amongst youth in the community.[24] The projects are connected with the Red Cross. Furthermore, many schools have started Mediation in Schools projects where the objects are similar to the object mentioned above. Both Mediation on the Streets and Mediation in Schools are peer-to-peer mediation and are examples of mediation independently of the criminal justice system.

Regardless of the offender's age, the voluntary nature of the

23 http://www.konfliktraadet.no/no/info/Felles/om/statistikk/ (Last accessed 10 November 2010).

24 http://www.salto.oslo.kommune.no (Last accessed 10 November 2010). This website, although mainly in Norwegian, also has a few pages in English explaining the projects.

participation will be secured to a greater degree in cases in which restorative justice is used independently of the criminal justice system. One might say that these arrangements are restorative justice in its 'purest form': it is probable that the offender's only rationale to participate is that he or she wants to contribute to restore the offence he or she has committed. Where a restorative justice arrangement is a part of the criminal justice system, there will often be a hidden treat that may influence the offender's consent to participate in such an arrangement: participation may be caused by a wish or hope for a more lenient penal sanction or no penal sanction at all. Furthermore, the offender's consent to participate is also seen as important in obtaining a positive result in the restorative justice arrangements. Diverting cases fully from the criminal justice system may reduce the cost per unit case as well, but as far as I know this possible benefit of these programmes is not estimated in Norway.

5.4.3 Referral to restorative justice arrangements at pre-court stage – stage (2)

As in many European countries[25] restorative justice has tradition-ally mostly been used in Norway after referrals made by the pros-ecution authority at pre-court stage. The prosecution authority refers more than 80 per cent of the cases in the mediation board.[26] These numbers also include civil cases where the offender has not reached the minimum age of criminal responsibility and cases where no criminal offence has been committed. The main group of defendants in 2009 was 15–17 years old.[27] About 28 per cent of the defendants were in the 15–17 age group, and ca. 16 per cent of the defendants were in the 12–14 age group.[28] Criminal cases are referred in accordance with the Criminal Proceedings Act § 71a

25   Council of Europe Publishing, *Rebuilding community connections – mediation and restorative justice*, p. 23.
26   K.K. Paus, *Restorative Justice i Norden, regelverk og iverksetting* in *Restorative Justice in the Nordic Countries*, NSFK's 22nd Contact Seminar 2008, Reykjavik, Iceland, 31 October – 2 November.
27   In Norway the minimum age of criminal responsibility is 15 years old.
28   http://www.konfliktraadet.no/no/info/Felles/om/statistikk/ (Last accessed 10 November 2010).

both where the offender is a minor and where he or she is an adult. Such referrals shall be made only where there is sufficient evidence to charge the offender, the case is considered 'suitable' for referring and both the victim and the offender have consented. The gravity of the offences referred in accordance with Criminal Proceedings Act § 71a is in most cases less serious. In these cases restorative justice is used as an alternative to both criminal proceedings and a traditional sentence.

Where a case is referred to a restorative justice arrangement without prior criminal proceedings, the clarification of the norm and deciding what the facts of the case are left to the restorative justice arrangement. This might have some disadvantages further discussed in Section 5.4.8, but the procedure might probably be more easily justifiable where the case is less serious than in these cases. As the prosecution authority is referring the cases, the possibility of referring cases where no offence has been committed is also reduced by the authority's competence: although the prosecution authority has no competence to pass any sentences, the authority has knowledge in criminal law and should have a hand in avoiding referring cases where no offence has been committed. If someone finds themselves harmed, but no offence has been committed, they will have to get in touch with the mediation board themselves and the case will be handled as a civil case.

Diversion of the cases from the criminal justice system at an early stage may reduce the strain on the offender, regardless of the offender being a minor or an adult: not only a sentence, but also going through a criminal proceeding will put a strain on the offender, especially minors. Diversion will probably contribute as far as possible to avoiding stigmatisation of the child on the basis of the child's involvement in a criminal case. Nevertheless: one should not underestimate the strain put on the offender participating in victim–offender mediation or group conferences – facing the victim and dealing with the effects of the offence committed will take its toll on the offender. This strain the offender is put under is often pointed out to validate the use of restorative justice arrangements instead of traditional punitive sanctions, but the fact that participating in a restorative justice arrangement is seldom as easy as it intuitively sounds also calls for attention in the criminal cases referred to the mediation board in accordance with the Criminal

Proceedings Act § 71a. The principle of equality and the principle of proportionality may require that the measures imposed by the restorative justice arrangement are not too severe compared with the penal sanction that would have been imposed on the child if the case was not referred.

The different focus in traditional criminal proceedings and restorative justice arrangements may be a challenge to the assessment of proportionality – the response outlined in the restorative justice arrangement may be seen both as too severe or too lenient compared with what the outcome of a traditional criminal proceeding would have been. Circumstances that are important to the stakeholders might not be relevant in criminal proceedings. If such circumstances are emphasised in the restorative justice arrangement, one might see that the outcome of the restorative justice arrangement would not have been considered as proportionate in the traditional criminal justice system, even if it is seen as proportionate to the offence as it has been presented in the restorative justice arrangement. Antony Duff has pointed out that the assessment of proportionality should not be too severe: 'So whilst on this account we should not seek a strict proportionality between crime and reparation or make proportionality our positive aim, we must respect the demands of a rough and negative proportionality: the reparation must not be disproportionate in its severity to the seriousness of the crime.'[29] But even when we base the assessment of proportionality on a negative proportionality one can still ask whether it is correct to base this assessment on the information provided in the criminal proceedings and not on a wider set of information provided in a restorative justice arrangement.

Walgrave and Geudens point out that restorative proportionality and criminal proportionality are two different sorts of proportionality – and that they deviate significantly from each other. They show that restorative proportionality needs to be developed.[30] As mentioned above, (Section 5.3), the theoretical foundation

29 A. Duff, 'Restoration and Retribution' in A. von Hirsch, J. Roberts, A. E.
    Bottoms, K. Roach and M. Schiff (eds.), *Restorative Justice and Criminal Justice.
    Competing or Reconcilable Paradigms?* (Oxford and Portland, OR: Hart Publishing,
    2003), p. 57.
30 Walgrave and Geudens, 'The Restorative Proportionality of Community
    Service for Juveniles'.

for restorative justice needs to be developed in Norway as well. Whether it is necessary to develop a restorative proportionality depends on the starting point: is restorative justice supposed to be a part of the criminal justice system or should it develop as a separate, and alternative, paradigm? If restorative justice should develop as a separate alternative to criminal justice, there is certainly a need for developing a particular restorative proportionality. But if restorative justice should be, as it seems most adequate to categorise it in a comprehensive Norwegian criminal justice system, a part of the criminal justice system, the theoretical development should perhaps concentrate on how the outcome of a restorative justice process can fit into the criminal justice system without losing its restorative elements.

The principle of equality may call for equal treatment in criminal proceedings and restorative justice arrangements as well, and the principle of legality can also impose restrictions on which circumstances may be emphasised in criminal cases.

5.4.4 Restorative justice used parallel to prosecution – stage (3)?

Formally restorative justice arrangements are not used parallel to prosecution in Norway. This does not obstruct the offender and the victim in a criminal case from taking part in such an arrangement, regardless of their age. In a restorative justice arrangement the offender and the victim will most likely be able to talk about the offence in a way they will not be able to in the criminal proceedings: they may bring to light aspects of the crime that are important to them, but that may not be dealt with in court. The advantages and disadvantages of using restorative justice parallel to prosecution seem to be similar regardless of the offender's age.

In a report to the Norwegian parliament from the Ministry of Justice and Police, a group conference used in a homicide case is described.[31] In this case all the involved persons were closely related. The murderer was released from detention, and the relatives of the victim were afraid to meet him in the street. There were also rumours of revenge on both sides of the conflict.

31   St.meld. nr. 37 (2007-2008) *Straff som virker*, p. 161.

As the group conference was held before the criminal proceedings, it was prearranged that the participants should talk only about the consequences of the act after it happened. Both the counsel for the defendant and the public prosecutor participated in the group conference, but both had in advance stated that they would not use in court anything discussed in the conference.

As mentioned above, restorative justice arrangements are formally not used parallel to prosecution. If such arrangements are carried out after all, this brings up questions how both the court and the restorative justice arrangements should deal with the parallel courses. In my opinion the fact that the offender has shown willingness to participate in such an arrangement may be a mitigating circumstance when the court is passing its sentence. More problematic is how to handle the different approaches to exchanging information. In the criminal justice system the offender has the right to not to be compelled to testify against himself or to confess guilt.[32] In restorative justice arrangements an important premise for the process is that the offender is willing to explain what has happened. If a restorative justice arrangement is arranged parallel to prosecution, the situation may arise that the offender is reluctant to give information about the offence in the restorative justice arrangement. In the case mentioned above some of these possible problems were solved as both the counsel for the defendant and the public prosecutor affirmed in advance that they would not use any information from the group conference in court. It also shows that in this case the prosecution authority was very positive to a parallel path in the mediation board in addition to the criminal proceedings.

If the offender gives information in the restorative justice arrangement arranged by the mediation board, the mediator is bound by his professional secrecy, and he or she is prohibited from testifying about what the parties have admitted in the mediation or conference. The mediator cannot testify about this without the offender's and victim's consent, according to the National Mediation Service Act § 10, but the court can in some circumstances revoke the prohibition against testifying about other ques-

---

32   UN International Covenant on Civil and Political Rights (ICCPR) Article 14 (3)
(g) and ECHR Article 6.

tions in the case. Even if the mediator is prohibited from testifying, the victim is not – and this may give both the police and the court information about what the offender has admitted in a restorative justice arrangement.

5.4.5 Restorative justice used after conviction and before sentencing – stage (4)?

There has been no tradition of using restorative justice arrangements after conviction and before sentencing in Norway. One reason for this is probably that the main rule is that conviction and sentence are not two separate stages in the criminal proceedings.[33] A new proposition put forward in the White Paper NOU 2008: 15 may to some extent change the tradition of not using restorative justice arrangements in between conviction and sentencing, if it is implemented. A committee on juvenile delinquency has proposed introducing youth conferences as an alternative to prison in cases where the offender has not turned 18 at the time of the crime. The proposed sentence contains two parts: participating in the youth conference where a youth plan will be made, and carrying out the measures imposed in this youth plan. If this response is established, it will be the only penal response reserved for minors in Norway. The proposed response stands out as a non-custodial sentence (Section 5.4.6) but differs from other Norwegian non-custodial sentences in one sense: the case will always be sent back to the court for approval of the youth plan. The court will impose an alter-

---

33 These stages may be separated where there is any doubt concerning the mental state of the person indicted or the court finds that there are other reasons that make it desirable to do so, cf. the Criminal Procedure Act § 288. In addition the Court of Appeal sits with a jury when an appeal is brought against the assessment of evidence in relation to the issue of guilt and the appeal is concerned with a felony punishable pursuant to statute by imprisonment for a term exceeding six years, cf. the Criminal Procedure Act 288, Section 1. In the cases where the Court of Appeal sits with a jury, the conviction and sentence are two separate parts in the criminal proceedings. The cases where the Court of Appeal will sit with a jury are, however, even more restricted where the person charged was under 18 years of age when the felony was committed. In these cases the Court of Appeal will sit with a jury only where the prosecuting authority does not intend to propose, and the judgment appealed against has not imposed, a sentence of imprisonment for a term exceeding two years, cf. the Criminal Procedure Act § 352, Section 2.

native sentence in prison in all cases where youth conferences are imposed. If the court does not approve the youth plan made in the youth conference when the case is referred back to the court, the court will have to decide to what extent this alternative sentence shall be implemented. At this stage the court will have to decide on the significance of participating in a youth conference even if the youth plan is not considered good enough: the first part of the sentence will have been implemented even if the youth plan is not approved. When the alternative sentence is implemented the court will have to adjust the alternative sentence taking into account to what extent the primary sentence has been implemented. The final sentencing occurs at this point. This makes it not so far-fetched to systematise the response as restorative justice used after conviction and before sentencing. In these cases restorative justice will be an alternative to a traditional sentence, but not an alternative to traditional criminal proceedings.

By proposing a restorative justice arrangement monitored by the court, the Committee on juvenile delinquency has opened up the possibility of imposing youth conferences in more severe cases than those that are referred to the mediation board today. In this case this means that restorative justice can be used where a minor has committed a crime of violence, sexual crime, burglary or aggravated robbery.[34] Today juvenile offenders in these cases will most likely be sentenced to prison or at best community service. The judicial review is at the same time supposed to secure the principles of proportionality, legal authority and equality before the law.

Reducing the use of prison sentences where the offender is under age is an advantage in itself, as serving a prison sentence is clearly negative for juvenile offenders. The fact that it has not been found that prison reduces the juvenile offenders' recidivism increases the problems of using such a penal sanction. In an experiment run by the Norwegian government in four large Norwegian cities different approaches to juvenile delinquency have been tried, based on the principles of restorative justice. The proposition in NOU 2008: 15 is based on these experiments and especially the experiment in one of these cities, Trondheim, where the project has shown a high level of

---

34   NOU 2008: 15 *Barn og straff – utviklingsstøtte og kontroll*, pp. 148–149.

participation in the measures put forward by the youth conference, a high level of satisfaction both among offenders and victims, and a reduced recidivism among offenders.[35]

According to the proposition the juvenile offenders referred to youth conferences will still have to go through criminal proceedings, which are still going to put a strain on the offender. As shown in Section 5.4.2 it is necessary to clarify the norms and guarantee the rights of the offender in such proceedings.

Introducing restorative justice in more severe cases is also to introduce questions that do not occur in less severe cases. In more severe cases the possibility of the offender being remanded in custody is increased. As mentioned above in Section 5.2 a juvenile offender cannot be remanded in custody unless it is especially necessary. If a minor has been in custody, this will nowadays be taken into account when the sentence is passed. Both the principle of proportionality and equality before the law call for this also to be taken into account if a case is referred to a youth conference. Furthermore, the importance of securing that the outcome of the restorative justice arrangement (according to the proposition: the youth plan) is sufficiently followed up and carried out increases in accordance with the level of seriousness of the case. If victims experience that the results of the restorative process are not realised in real life, there is a risk that the general attitude to participating in such processes would turn negative.

5.4.6 Restorative justice as a part of and/or in addition to non-custodial sentences – stage (5)

Traditionally, restorative justice arrangements have not been used very often as a part of, or in addition to, non-custodial sentences in Norway. This seems, however, to be changing. Since 2003 the court can prescribe mediation as a condition of a suspended sentence, both where the offender is a minor and where he/she is an adult, in accordance with the Penal Code § 53 no. 3 (h). These cases will be referred to the mediation board. The court is not constrained

---

35   Ø. Kvello and C. Wendelborg: *Prosessevaluering av det treårige prosjektet: Oppfølgingsteam for unge lovbrytere i Kristiansand, Oslo, Stavanger og Trondheim* (Trondheim: NTNU Samfunnsforskning AS, 2009).

to impose mediation as the only condition to such a sentence. The court can select from among a wide range of conditions. A suspended sentence can also be used in addition to an immediate sentence. This makes it possible to both be sentenced to prison and to have one's case referred to the mediation board. The courts' competence to impose mediation as a condition of a suspended sentence is limited only if either the victim or the offender has not consented. Forty-one cases were referred to the mediation board by the courts as a condition of a suspended sentence in 2007.[36] This makes a total of 0.44 per cent of the total number of cases received by the mediation board this year and 0.90 per cent of the criminal cases received this year. In these cases restorative justice is not an alternative to criminal proceedings. Restorative justice is instead, as a rule, an alternative to a traditional sentence, but can, as shown, be a supplement to an immediate sentence.

Furthermore, the correctional service can impose mediation as a part of community service. In these cases restorative justice is an alternative to a traditional sentence. Forty-four cases were referred to the mediation board by the correctional service in 2007.[37] This makes a total of 0.48 per cent of the total number of cases, and 0.87 per cent of the criminal cases in that year. In total 1.8 per cent of the criminal cases referred to the mediation board in 2007 were cases where mediation was a part of a non-custodial sentence.

The severity in these cases will most often be between the cases referred to the mediation boards by the prosecution authority and the cases where the minor is sentenced immediately. In these cases the courts will consider whether an offence has been committed, but in contrast to the proposition of youth conferences (Section 5.4.5) the courts in these cases will not be able to make a judicial review of the proportionality between the offence and the deal made in a victim–offender mediation or conference.

36 Paus, *Restorative Justice i Norden, regelverk og iverksetting.*
37 *Ibid.*

5.4.7 Restorative justice in prison, post-sentence or pre-release – stage (6)?

The Norwegian government has expressed the view that restorative justice may also be used when the offender is imprisoned.[38] There has been an experiment at a prison in Arendal using restorative justice in such cases. The evaluation shows that the mediation board played an important rehabilitative role in the prison. It also showed that spreading knowledge about mediation and restorative justice to the staff might have a positive effect.[39]

Where mediation is used independently of the criminal justice system or where the offender is imprisoned, restorative justice is neither an alternative to traditional criminal proceedings nor an alternative to traditional sentencing – the offender will have to deal with the strain both of these may put on him or her. In these cases restorative justice programmes are instead a supplement to the traditional criminal proceedings and sentencing. As in the cases where restorative justice arrangements take place independently of the criminal justice system, the voluntary nature of the participation will to a larger degree be secured in such cases than in cases pending in the criminal justice system.

5.4.8 Swapping criminal justice for restorative justice: The limits of restorative justice

Restorative justice can be used as an alternative to a traditional sentence or as both an alternative to criminal proceedings and a traditional sentence. Where criminal proceedings take place, but restorative justice is replacing a traditional sentence, restorative justice is *supplementing* criminal justice. Where restorative justice is used without prior criminal proceedings, restorative justice is a true *alternative* to criminal justice. As presented above, restorative justice is most often used as an alternative to criminal justice in the Norwegian juvenile justice system, either occurring independently of the criminal justice system or by referral at pre-court stage, see Sections 5.4.2 and 5.4.3. A circumstance that may have a negative

38　St.meld. nr. 37 (2007-2008) *Straff som virker*, p. 164.

39　Ida Hydle, with contributions from Arne Værland and Ingrid Kristine Hasund, *Konfliktråd i fengsel. Rapport fra et prosjekt 2003/2004* (Kristiansand: Høgskolen i Agder, 2004).

impact on such restorative justice arrangements is the fact that in these cases the question whether an offence has been committed will not be tested by the court, as restorative justice is used without a traditional criminal proceeding ahead of the referral to the mediation board.[40] This seems to be in accordance with the view of Nils Christie in his aforementioned article: he wants to let the parties of a conflict decide for themselves what they think is relevant in the case – not only when it comes to deciding how restitution will be made for the offence, but also when deciding whether an offence has been committed. Christie wants to take the conflicts out of the hands of the experts (especially the lawyers) and bring it back to its stakeholders – and replace the traditional criminal justice system with a system based on a victim-oriented and lay-oriented court. He argues that this will be an opportunity for clarification of the norm: it will be an opportunity for a continuous discussion of what represents, or should represent, the law of the land.[41]

Christie's argumentation is flattering: perhaps both the offender and the victim will leave the victim–offender mediation or the group conference with a revised view of what the community accepts from them or not. Maybe this process will show that the offender is not such a terrifying person as the victim believed in advance, and maybe this knowledge will have an influence on the view of the parties of the conflict on whether the offender has acted in discrepancy with the norms in the community. Restorative justice arrangements have shown good results in many ways[42] and it is tempting to accept to hand over the entire process, the clarification of the norm as well as the finding of the facts, to the restorative justice arrangement as well. In the restorative justice arrangements

---

40 Where cases are referred to a restorative justice arrangement at pre-court stage, the referrals will be filtered by the police and this should decrease the possibility of handling as criminal cases those cases where it is obvious that no crime has been committed.

41 N. Christie, 'Conflicts as Property', *The British Journal of Criminology*, 17 (1), 1977, pp. 1–15, esp. p. 12.

42 Umbreit, Vos, Coates and Lightfoot give an overview of evaluations of victim satisfaction, offender satisfaction and recidivism in cases where victim–offender mediation and group conferences are used. M.S. Umbreit, B. Vos, R.B. Coates and E. Lightfoot, 'Restorative Justice in the Twenty-First Century: A Social Movement Full of Opportunities and Pitfalls', *Marquette Law Review*, 89, (2005), pp. 251–304.

occurring independently of the criminal justice system this has been done – as there have been no criminal proceedings previous to the participation in these arrangements. The stakeholders will have to decide what harm has actually been done. A special feature of some of these arrangements is that they mediate where one person has harmed another in smaller communities, as in school (Mediation in School) or in the local environment (Mediation on the Streets). This is probably most likely to be the situation in most of the civil cases concerning minor 'offenders' who have not turned 15. It is hardly controversial to assume that minors under 15 years are more closely connected to their local environment than adults – and that their offences most often will be committed in this local environment.

In small communities the offender and the victim will often have to coexist in the aftermath of the crime. This makes it important not only to clarify the facts, but also to clarify the norms, the offender, and the victim in between. In addition, this may increase the information about the norms to their local environment. The people in the participants' local environment will learn from both the victim and the offender what has happened and how they dealt with it. In larger communities where the citizens do not know each other so well or perhaps even not at all – and where the victim and offender perhaps even will not ever meet again, the importance of clarifying the norms in between them is not as high as in a smaller community. On the other hand, in such a larger community – the society at large – it may be of a greater importance to clarify the norms at a higher level: to all citizens. In this society the victim and offender will not be able to bring forth the same information to all their fellow citizens as in a smaller community – the mechanism of getting to know what has happened and how the stakeholders have dealt with it is not so well developed here. In these larger communities one might experience that leaving the stakeholders to define what the norms are might result not so much in clarity as in confusion. Different participants in different restorative justice arrangements might end up with different results when asking whether an action has been in discrepancy with a norm. One can argue that everyone has a common understanding of some breaches of norms: such as one shall not murder or one shall not steal,[43] but how would the participants of a restorative justice arrangement consider a person who has given his or her child a smack, a person who has killed his or her mother out of mercy – or a group of minors who have played with the thought of making a bomb? It is in these circumstances that the criminal justice system has it strengths: the system is made for clarifying norms; the lawyers study the norms before they are authorised to pass any judgements and the hierarchical construction of the courts encourages coherence in the norms. The disadvantages that arise when the norms are not clarified relate both to adults and minors, but are probably particularly significant where the offender is a minor: minors will need more guidance than adults will in what is acceptable behaviour. Coherence of the norms will be conducive in securing both the principle of equality before the law and the principle of proportionality. If the norms do not cohere, one lacks a joint starting point to determine the question of proportionality.

Furthermore, the criminal proceedings play an important role in securing the fundamental rights of the defendant in a criminal case. The European Convention for the Protection of Human Rights and Fundamental Freedoms (ECHR) sets forth such fundamental rights. Article 6 of the convention states that everyone is entitled to a fair hearing by *an independent and impartial trial* established by law in the determination of any criminal charge against him (Article 6 (1)), and everyone charged with a criminal offence shall be *presumed innocent until proved guilty in accordance with the law*. Article 7 of the convention states that no one shall be held guilty of any criminal offence on account of any act or omission which did not *constitute a criminal offence under national or international law at the time when it was committed*. These rights exist, in addition, to secure that the clarification of norms should be left to the courts, securing that the courts shall decide what the facts are in criminal cases. It is a principle of legal authority.

The ECHR was ratified in the aftermath of the Second World War, but these rights have grown from the political philosophy of the Age of the Enlightenment, where the principles of legal author-

---

43   Also a part of the basic rules in the world religions (i.e. the Ten Commandments in the Bible (Exodus 20: 1–17) and Koran Suras 5. 32 and 5. 38).

ity, equality before the law and proportionality were essential to protect citizens from brutal and arbitrary sentences. These principles are today important parts of the *Rechtsstaat*[44] (rule of law). It is not claimed that these rights cannot at all be taken care of in restorative justice arrangements, but handing over the clarification of the norm and the decision on what has occurred to restorative justice arrangements *may* result in a neglect of the fundamental rights mentioned above, which calls for the utmost caution in doing so: one should not make such dramatic changes to the criminal justice system without a comprehensive debate on these issues.

In some of the arrangements mentioned in Section 5.4.2 above, it is probably fairer to say that the arrangements have undertaken the clarification of the norm themselves, and not that this has been handed over by the Norwegian governmental authorities. If someone wants to leave it to private arrangements to decide whether he or she has acted in accordance with moral rights, this will, as a basic rule, not be in discrepancy with the fundamental rights of the citizens.[45] Furthermore, the fact that the offender has consented to participate in the restorative justice arrangements and that he or she at any time can withdraw from the arrangement indicates that the arrangements clarifying the norm are justifiable in these cases. Participating in e.g. Mediation on the Streets or Mediation in Schools, where the offender has turned 15 and can be subjected to criminal proceedings, does not obstruct such later proceedings either. In addition, these cases are very often less serious.

Broadening the scope of the restorative justice arrangements may lead to conflicts with the fundamental rights of the defendant – especially if this includes handing over from criminal proceedings to restorative justice arrangements the clarification of the norm and deciding what the facts are. The circumstances mentioned above, especially the offenders' consent, and that the cases are less serious, may perhaps justify handing over – to some extent – the clarification of the norm, and deciding what the facts are, to restorative justice arrangements. One may argue that cases where the crime committed is a minor crime, the lack of the guarantee of criminal

---

44   See footnote 2, Chapter 1.
45   There may be exceptions here, if a private arrangement imposes comprehensive measures in order to 'punish'.

proceedings in the criminal justice system will not be so obvious. In my opinion, the advantages of using restorative justice arrangements indicate that such arrangements should be used as often as possible where the offender is a minor and the offence is less serious. The disadvantages of not having prior criminal proceedings indicate, on the other hand, that it is necessary at some point to strike a balance where the offence is of such a serious nature that it should be handled by the courts to clarify the norms, before it is referred to a restorative justice arrangement, even if going through criminal proceedings might put a strain on the offender. To me it seems as if the proposition put forward in NOU 2008: 15 (as explained in Section 5.4.5) is a step in the direction where the necessity of judicial review is taken care of, although the option of an increased use of restorative justice arrangements where more serious offences have been made is offered. In the next section I shall discuss this proposition further.

5.5   Future development – more restorative justice arrangements? Are there any hazards?

One can see that there exist many different restorative justice arrangements in Norway today with regard to dealing with youth crime: the most common is mediation after referral to the mediation board made by the prosecution authority where minors have committed less serious crimes. At some of the other stages of the criminal proceedings, such as part of non-custodial sentences, the use of restorative justice arrangements is not as widespread but seems to be growing. An interesting trend in the Norwegian juvenile justice system is that in more severe cases the use of restorative justice arrangements seems to be changing from being a part of another sentence to becoming a melting-pot of different responses toward juvenile offenders. This seems to promote the use of restorative justice.

The juvenile justice system in Norway has for years been characterised by numerous experiments both by local and government directives. A number of these experiments are based on principles of restorative justice, but the experiments also combine the restorative justice arrangements with other rehabilitative elements such as measures initiated by the child welfare authorities and measures known from the criminal justice system.

The proposal put forward in NOU 2008: 15 is founded on these experiments, but it also goes further. Youth conferences are proposed, regulated by laws, and monitored by the courts. The proposed youth conference itself is based on the principles of restorative justice. The youth plan, proposed in the youth conference, is supposed to contain restorative, rehabilitative and punitive elements. In the following I shall describe the details of this proposal.

In accordance with the proposal a non-pecuniary compensation can be agreed. This is a well-known – and a fundamental – part of restorative justice arrangements. It nevertheless seems as if the proposal is in conflict with the principles of restorative justice in two ways: it is proposed that it shall not be possible to agree to pay a traditional pecuniary compensation. Assessment of such compensation is left to the court. In addition it is proposed that the consent of the victim is not mandatory in order to refer a case to a youth conference. The youth conference is motivated by the principle of equality: the offender's possibility to sustain a non-custodial sentence should not depend solely on the victim's consent. The importance of the victim's participation is nevertheless strongly emphasised in the proposal. It is pointed out that the victim will need to be given information and support by the mediation board.[46]

In addition, the proposal offers the option of community service to be a part of the youth plan. As mentioned above (section 5.3), this is traditionally not seen as a restorative measure in Norway, but is rather, due to the process of passing such a sentence and the contents of the community service, seen as a punitive measure. In accordance with the proposal, an officer from the correctional services shall always be a part of a youth conference. Implementing this part of the proposal may perhaps lead to a higher degree of restorative elements in imposing community service in these cases – in practice. Other possible measures proposed, such as abstaining from alcohol or other intoxicants, reporting to the police, restrictions on place of residence, instructions to be at work or at school, avoid certain persons and to stay at home at certain fixed times

46 NOU 2008: 15 *Barn og straff – utviklingsstøtte og kontroll*, pp. 155–56.

are already known from the Norwegian criminal justice system.

Additionally, action programmes worked out to prevent criminal acts can be a part of the youth plan. In Norway such programmes are used both in prison and as a part of non-custodial sentences, but it is probably most appropriate to consider such programmes as rehabilitative. Other rehabilitative measures, such as placing the minors in an institution run by the Child Welfare Service, might be a part of the youth plan as well.

This means that the youth conference, if introduced into the Norwegian juvenile justice system, will have access to a wide range of measures. To a great extent this seems to be in accordance with the UN Economic and Social Council's resolution: ECO-SOC Resolution 2002/12 Article 3: 'Restorative outcomes include responses and programmes such as reparation, restitution and community service, aimed at meeting the individual and collective needs and responsibilities of the parties and at achieving the reintegration of the victim and the offender.'

All in all, the proposal has received support from the bodies entitled to comment on it.[47] It seems that having measures accessible that make it possible to customise the response to the single juvenile offender have been long awaited. The positive reception of the proposals and the assumption that the proposal is in accordance with the ECOSOC resolution do not take away the necessity of asking whether the accessibility of such a wide range of measures is justifiable.

The measures in the youth plan will be imposed by the youth conference, approved by the court, monitored by a team chosen from the participants in the youth conference and a co-ordinator employed by the mediation board and monitored by the court. The seriousness of the cases referred to the youth conference will be grave and the child who has committed an offence might feel under pressure to accept extensive measures to avoid an immediate sentence. In my opinion it is important that neither the youth conference nor the court approving the youth plan falls into the well-meant temptation of imposing too many measures in such

---

47   http://www.regjeringen.no/dep/jd/dok/hoeringer/hoeringsdok/2008/horing-
--nou-2008-15-om-barn-og-straff/horingsuttalelser.html?id=544533 (Last
accessed 10 November 2010).

a way that good intentions make the child endure more extensive measures than a traditional sentence does. As mentioned above, the mere participation in a restorative justice programme will put the child under strain.

Many of the juvenile offenders in cases referred to a youth conference will have a number of unsolved problems that one can assume play a part in the child's criminal conduct (so-called risk factors).[48] Studies show that reducing the child's risk factors reduces the chances of the child's reoffending. It is reasonable to believe that knowledge of a child's risk factors will lead to a desire to do something about such underlying problems. Having a wide range of measures accessible makes this possible. A red flag should be raised immediately when the measures imposed are of a comprehensive nature. Such measures cannot be brought about in every case where a child has committed a crime. The measures imposed must fulfil a minimum of proportionality to the offence committed. The proposal from the Committee on juvenile delinquency has to some extent taken this into account when the new response proposed is reserved for grave offences where being sentenced to prison is the alternative to referring the case to a youth conference.

Even though restorative justice arrangements have many positive qualities, opening up the possibility of restorative justice becoming part of the juvenile justice system requires that these programmes to some extent adjust to the guiding principles in the criminal justice system. Opening up the possibility of restorative justice programmes to impose comprehensive measures on the minor increases the importance of this, even where the offender has consented. The fact that many measures are imposed with good intentions, because one believes such measures will keep the child from reoffending, also makes it important to have a system that is able to put the brake on where the measures are too comprehensive in proportion to the offence committed. History has shown that good intentions sometimes just may not be enough. The fact that the restorative justice process itself seems to have good results in preventing reoffending is also an argument not to impose comprehensive measures on the juvenile offender – risking that the offend-

48 T. Andreassen, *Behandling av ungdom i institusjoner. Hva sier forskningen?* (Oslo: Kommuneforlaget, 2003) pp. 29ff.

ers stop consenting to take part in restorative justice programmes as an alternative to prison sentences, and instead choose to serve a sentence in prison.

Claiming that restorative justice programmes have to adjust themselves to the criminal justice system to become a part of criminal justice systems, as an alternative to a traditional sentence, is perhaps to undermine the ideology of restorative justice – being a counter-reaction to this system. But maybe it is possible to see this as taking the best part of two systems, creating a better alternative in the treatment of juvenile offenders.

References

Andreassen, T., *Behandling av ungdom i institusjoner. Hva sier forskningen?* (Oslo: Kommuneforlaget, 2003).

Christie, N., 'Conflicts as Property', *The British Journal of Criminology*, 17 (1), 1977, pp. 1–15.

Council of Europe Publishing, *Rebuilding Community Connections – Mediation and Restorative Justice*, written by Ivo Aertsen, Robert Mackay, Christa Pelikan, Martin Wright and Jolien Willemsens for the Council of Europe (Strasbourg: 2004).

Duff, A., 'Restoration and Retribution' in A. von Hirsch, J. Roberts, A.E. Bottoms, K. Roach and M. Schiff (eds.), *Restorative Justice and Criminal Justice. Competing or Reconcilable Paradigms?* (Oxford and Portland, OR: Hart Publishing, 2003), p. 57.

Hagerup, F., *Forhandlinger ved Den Norske Kriminalistforenings første møte i oktober 1892* (Kristiania: Aschehoug, 1895).

Hauge, R., *Straffens begrunnelser* (Oslo: Universitetsforlaget, 1996).

Hydle, I., with contributions from A. Værland and I. K. Hasund, *Konfliktråd i fengsel. Rapport fra et prosjekt 2003/2004* (Kristiansand: Høgskolen i Agder, 2004).

Kvello, Ø., and Wendelborg, C., *Prosessevaulering av det treårige prosjektet: Oppfølgingsteam for unge lovbrytere i Kristiansand, Oslo, Stavanger og Trondheim* (Trondheim: NTNU Samfunnsforskning AS, 2009).

Marshall, T.F., *Restorative Justice: an Overview* (London: [British] Home Office, Research and Statistics Directorate, 1999).

Paus, K.K., *Restorative Justice i Norden, regelverk og iverksetting* in *Restorative Justice in the Nordic Countries, NSfK's 22nd Contact Seminar 2008, Reykjavik, Iceland. 31 October–2 November.*

Umbreit, M.S., 'Holding Juvenile Offenders Accountable: A Restorative Justice Perspective', *Juvenile and Family Court Journal*, 1995, pp. 31–42.

Umbreit, M.S., Vos, B., Coates, R.B., and Lightfoot, E., 'Restorative

Justice in the Twenty-First Century: A Social Movement Full of Opportunities and Pitfalls', *Marquette Law Review*, 89, (2005), pp. 251–304.

Walgrave, L., 'Restoration in Youth Justice', *Crime and Justice*, 31, 2004.

Walgrave, L., and Geudens, H., 'The Restorative Proportionality of Community Service for Juveniles', *European Journal of Crime, Criminal Law and Criminal Justice*, 1996, pp. 361–80.

Legal sources

NOU 1985: 3 *Tiltak for ungdom med atferdsvansker.*

NOU 2008: 15 *Barn og straff – utviklingsstøtte og kontroll.*

Riksadvokatens rundskriv: *Mål og prioriteringer for straffesaksbehandlingen i politiet – 2010.*

St.meld. 37 (2007–2008) *Straff som virker – mindre kriminalitet – tryggere samfunn (Kriminalomsorgsmelding).*

The Committee of Ministers, Council of Europe: *Recommendation NO. R (99) 19 of the Committee of Ministers to Member States concerning mediation in penal matters.*

United Nations Economic and Social Council *Resolution* ECOSOC *Resolution 2002/12.*

6. Striking a balance between justice and peace: Restorative justice in states of transition

ELIZABETH BAUMANN

6.1 Introductory remarks

6.1.1 The problems at stake

The relationship between retributive and restorative justice is a pressing subject for the enforcement of international criminal law after war and civil strife. The main questions that occur are three-fold: (1) Under what conditions are criminal prosecutions mandatory or only permissible? (2) If prosecutions are permissible, to what extend does international criminal law allow for a restorative approach? (3) Which categories of restorative approaches may fit the demands of international criminal law? This article will consider whether the global combat against impunity for international crimes, under the scheme of an exceptional post-conflict discretion, allows certain non-punitive measures in order to maintain peace, reconciliation, and the restoration of the broken society.

The course of restorative justice may contribute to bridging the gap between the categorical demand of criminal trials and more flexible answers that can provide reconciliation. The restorative elements could be exemptions from prosecution on the conditions of the full disclosure of truth before a truth commission, compensation to the victims, and rehabilitation of the perpetrators to society. Although it is uncertain under what conditions restorative elements can be lawfully included in the enforcement of international criminal law, the current conceptualisation of the duty to prosecute does not exclude carefully crafted amnesties under certain criteria of validity.[1] Specifically, truth commissions that constitute serious attempts to investigate and disclose the past, publicise their findings, generate a space for victims' harm and include the offenders' recognition of the crime and apology, are regarded as principled compromises on the question of punishment or impunity.[2] None the less, the consistency of such a hybrid legal concept relies not only on an extensive definition of what measures there are that can serve the interest of justice, but also on the development of clear legal procedures for the key elements of the peace versus justice balance.[3] In this respect, a restorative choice, when it appears as an exemption from criminal trials, has to comply with specific legal criteria. The national process must be genuine, sincere, in good faith, open and effective. As argued by Robinson: 'One should consider the balance between the extent of the departure for full prosecutions, *i.e.* the quality of the measures taken and the severity of the factors necessitating a deviation, to decide whether a society has done everything possible to advance accountability-related goals.'[4] Ambos introduces the threefold *proportionality test* as the methodological tool, developed by the German Constitutional Court[5] and further Alexy and his *Rule of Balancing*.[6] Legal criteria suitable for defining exceptions from criminal prosecution should accordingly address the appropriateness, necessity and proportionality of the conduct.[7]

---

1   Anja Seibert-Fohr, *Prosecuting Serious Human Rights Violations* (Oxford University Press, 2009), pp. 285–89. See also Louise Mallinder, *Amnesty, Human Rights and Political Transition* (Oxford: Hart Publishing, 2008), pp. 409–13.

2   For a study in restorative elements, see Nancy Amoury Combs, *Guilty Pleas in International Criminal Law: Constructing a Restorative Approach* (Palo Alto, CA: Stanford University Press, 2007), pp. 21–26.

3   *E.g.* Kai Ambos, 'The Legal Framework of Transitional Justice: A Systematic Study with a Special Focus on the Role of the ICC' in K. Ambos, J. Large, and M. Wierda (eds.), *Building a Future on Peace and Justice: Studies in Transitional Justice, Peace and Development* (Berlin: Springer, 2010).

4   Darryl Robinson, 'Serving the Interest of Justice: Amnesties, Truth Commissions and the International Criminal Court', *European Journal of International Law* (2003), pp. 481–505, at p. 497.

5   Erdölbevorratung, 16.03.1971, BVerfGE [Decision of the German Constitutional Court] 30, 292, p. 316.

6   Ambos, 'The Legal Framework of Transitional Justice', para. 19. R. Alexy, *Theorie der Grundrechte* (Baden-Baden: Nomos, 1985).

7   Ambos, 'The Legal Framework of Transitional Justice', paras. 19–21.

6.1.2 *A conceptualisation within the legal order of transitional justice*

The issue goes to the heart of the post-conflict justice or transitional justice, under which the transition from repression and violence itself is a goal. Regarded as essential for sustainable peace, transitional justice as a part of *jus post bellum* has since early 1990 become a virtually inherent part of the enforcement of international peace and security, especially as a part of the UN paradigm.[8] According to *The Encyclopaedia of Genocide and Crimes against Humanity*, transitional justice refers to 'a field of activity and inquiry focused on how societies address legacies of past human rights abuses, mass atrocity, or other forms of severe social trauma, including genocide or civil war, in order to build a more democratic, just or peaceful future'.[9] As defined by the UN Secretary-General, transitional justice is connected to a certain period of national change. In order to accommodate this change, transitional justice allows for a wide range of legal tools of both a retributive and restorative character:

> The notion of transitional justice comprises the full range of processes and mechanisms associated with a society's attempt to come to terms with a legacy of large-scale past abuses, in order to ensure accountability, serve justice, and achieve reconciliation. These may include either judicial and non-judicial mechanisms, with differing levels of international involvement (or none at all) and individual prosecutions, reparations, truth-seeking, institutional reform, vetting and dismissals, or a combination thereof.[10]

The concept of 'transitional justice' as described above is later affirmed in the annual report of 2009 of the UN High Commissioner for Human Rights.[11] The transitional concept also applies to ongoing conflicts.

8   The concept of 'transitional justice' consists of 'both judicial and non-judicial processes and mechanisms, such as truth-seeking, prosecution initiatives, reparations programmes, institutional reform, or an appropriate combination thereof', UN Doc. A/HCR/12/18.

9   *The Encyclopedia of Genocide and Crimes against Humanity* (London: Macmillan Reference USA, 2004). Vol. 3, at 1045–47.

10   UN Security Council, *The Rule of Law and Transitional Justice in Conflict and Post-Conflict Societies. Report of the Secretary-General*, S/2004/616, 23 August 2004.

11   UN DOC, A/HCR/12/18, 6 August 2009, *Annual Report of the United Nations High Commissioner for Human Rights* (...), 'Analytical Study on Human Rights and Transitional Justice', para. 3.

The term assumes two key conditions, the concept of justice in a broader form than criminal justice and the concept of transition, as a major political transformation, both the historical moments of turning, and the long-term process towards peace and democracy. In this process, restorative justice in the sense of healing and repair of all parties – the victims, offenders and society at large – may serve as a valuable complement to retributive systems, although, in the perspectives of international criminal law, within a narrowed scope. Such complements could release the international community from the fatigue of founding and running extremely costly international criminal proceedings and contribute to closing the impunity gap that surfaces from selected show trials. This is especially relevant, as the contributions from these international trials for the restoration of the rule of law in the injured society are contested.[12]

In order to establish sustainable peace, four major dimensions of justice may be favourably addressed: legal, transitional, distributive, and restorative justice.[13] Legal justice, typically criminal prosecutions, refers to the formal rule of law institutions designed to maintain the rule of law and deliver justice. Transitional justice refers mainly to the short-term and often temporary judicial and non-judicial mechanisms and processes that address serious human rights violations, war crimes, and crimes against humanity committed in armed conflict. Distributive justice seeks to address the underlying causes of conflict. Restorative justice places strong emphasis on the restoration of relationships between offenders, victims, and the community. The question of legitimacy depends on the appropriateness of these conducts.

The familiar dilemmas of transitional justice, formulated as 'no peace without justice', 'peace or justice', 'trading justice for peace' refer to the post-conflict states' ability (or inability) to deal with

12   A critical view of the ICTR is expressed by Jose Alvarez in 'Crimes of the State/ Crimes of Hate: Lessons from Rwanda', *Yale Journal of International Law*, 24 (1999) pp. 365–484. Alvarez doubts that individual criminal prosecutions effectively address the problematic fact that the perpetrators of the genocide represent a substantial part of one of the ethnic groups of the populations.

13   Jon Elster, 'Justice, Truth, Peace', in Morten Bergsmo and Pablo Kalmanovitz (eds.), *Law in Peace Negotiations*, FICHL Publication Series No. 5 (Peace Research Institute Oslo (PRIO), 2009) pp. 21–28.

past atrocities in an appropriate way.[14] Consequently, its success depends not only on establishing criminal accountability, but also on the capability of contributing to reconciliation and the restoration of the national state. The quest for justice must be balanced with the interest of peace.[15] For this reason, the transitional justice system entails both judicial and non-judicial elements. Indeed, even if a duty for states to prosecute the offenders most responsible for the core international crimes may have reached the limit of customary international law, the peacemaking practice and reconstruction of war-torn societies include instruments like truth commissions combined with conditional amnesties.[16]

The choice between prosecutions in the sense of retributive justice or restorative options will probably follow different tracks of legal rationale. On the one hand, criminal justice will contribute to commonly acknowledged objectives of human rights protection, such as deterrence and incapacitation. Nevertheless, as noted by Kritz, the risk of imposing 'imperfect justice' in innumerable transitions of post-conflict countries is nearly inevitable, because their criminal justice systems time and again are dysfunctional: 'Criminal justice systems are designed for societies in which the violations of the law are the exception, not when violations of the law become the rule.'[17] On the other hand, restorative justice involves a community-based model of justice that places strong emphasis on the restoration of relationships between offenders, victims, and the community. None the less, restorative justice may trigger the regime of 'impunity' amnesties, foreclosing criminal prosecutions and shielding the perpetrators from punishment. As

14　See, *e.g.* Ruti Teitel, *Transitional Justice* (Oxford University Press, 2000), p. 6: 'The conception of justice in periods of political change is extraordinary and constructivist; it is alternately constituted by a constitutive of the transitions. The conception of justice that emerges is contextualised and partial: What is deemed just is contingent and informed by prior injustice. Response to repressive rule informs the meaning of adherence to the rule of law.'

15　A recent example is the Colombia Constitutional Court Judgment of the Justice and Peace Law, Sentencia No. C370/2006, 18 May 2006.

16　For a comprehensive study, see Mallinder, *Amnesty, Human Rights and Political Transition,* Oxford: Hart Publishing, 2008.

17　Neil J. Kritz, 'Where We Are and How We Got Here: An Overview of the Developments in the Search for Justice and Reconciliation' in Alice H. Henkin (ed.), *The Legacy of Abuse: Confronting the Past, Facing the Future*, (Washington, DC: The Aspen Institute, 2002).

Teitel stated: 'Truth commissions emerged as impunity antidote and amnesty analogue.'[18] In a balanced conceptualisation, the choices described are more accurately between different legitimate modalities of accountability. Noticeably, large-scale impunity is not an option underpinned by international law. If the primary rationale of the state is to compromise the call for justice, the good faith criteria are per se absent.

These issues relate to the extended conceptual framework for international criminal law, which includes a broadened concept of justice. In this respect, restorative options under certain conditions could fulfil the state's duties to initiate national measures against impunity. With the entry into force of the Statute of the International Criminal Court (ICC), the issue certainly carries significant practical implications, as to whether and when national reconciliation involving amnesties will render a case inadmissible.[19] Under ICC Statute Articles 17 and 53, a case may prove inadmissible for the Court if such national conduct is the result of a genuine but fragile process aimed at peace and reconciliation, and prosecutions then will not serve 'the interests of justice'.[20]

6.1.3 Outline

In Part I, the access to renunciation from prosecutions is analysed in the context of conventional and customary international law and the jurisprudence of international criminal law and human rights law. The standards in favour of prosecutions are in particular the body of international criminal law (Section 6.2.1), the universal enforcement of accountability for international crimes (Section 6.2.2) and the duty for the states to prosecute (Section 6.2.3). Standards favouring non-punitive measures are *inter alia* the goals of reconciliation and peace (Section 6.2.4). The discussion emphasises the post-conflict exceptions and whether restorative justice may contribute to bridging the impunity gap (Section 6.2.5). The focus is especially on the compatibility between the anti-impunity regime and the broadened terms of justice (Section 6.2.6). A vital

18   Teitel, *Transitional Justice*, p. 79.
19   Robinson, 'Serving the Interest of Justice'.
20   *Ibid.*

condition is that non-punitive measures usually rely on the admissibility of amnesties (Section 6.3). In Part II, the advantage of the use of restorative elements in post-conflict societies, particularly truth commissions, is sketchily elaborated (Section 6.4). In Part III, attention is finally drawn to the post-conflict cases of Rwanda and Afghanistan. In the context of the duty to prosecute, the post-conflict exceptions and the balance between the interest of justice and peace, the text will discuss the role of Gacaca grassroots courts in Rwanda with jurisdiction for low-level offenders that emerged after the Rwandan genocide (Section 6.5), and the possibility for a similar approach in Afghanistan (Section 6.6). In Part IV, some conclusions are drawn from the analysis and discussions.

PART I: TRANSITIONAL JUSTICE AND POST-CONFLICT EXCEPTIONS

6.2   The legal standards of transitional justice

6.2.1 International criminal law: The enforcement of individual criminal liability for international crimes

International criminal law represents an international public order and draws upon notions, principles and legal constructs derived from international humanitarian law as well as human rights law.[21] Cassese defines the system of international criminal law as 'a body of international rules designed both to proscribe certain categories of conduct (war crimes, crimes against humanity, genocide, torture, aggression, terrorism) and to make those persons who engage in such conduct criminally liable'.[22] International criminal law thus identifies the individual liability for crimes against international law.[23] This development has radically changed the structure of

---

21 International criminal law has its sources not only in the laws of the national state, the statutes of the international court and international customary law, but also in the general principles of law. *Prosecutor* v. *Furundszija*, ICTY, No. IT9517/1T at 157157 (10 December 1998).

22 Antonio Cassese, *International Criminal Law* (Oxford University Press, 2008).

23 The Nuremberg Trials describe the relation between state responsibility and individual liability by pointing out that: 'Crimes against international law are

international law, from the voluntary nature to state responsibility and an internationalised *ordre public,* concerning interest belonging to the world at large. Moreover, the establishment of the international criminal tribunals has led to the evolution of a fully-fledged body of law.[24]

6.2.2 *The steps towards a universal scheme of prosecutions*

The global quest to end impunity after mass atrocities took a revolutionary turning point fifty years after the Nuremberg and Tokyo tribunals. The UN Security Council, in the wake of the post-cold war era, acting under Chapter VII of the UN Charter, established the ad hoc tribunals, the International Criminal Tribunal for the former Yugoslavia (ICTY) and the International Criminal Tribunal for Rwanda (ICTR).[25] The Security Council, when establishing the ICTR in 1994, underlined the close relationship between justice and peace: 'Convinced that in the particular circumstances of Rwanda, the prosecutions of persons responsible for serious violations of international humanitarian law would (...) contribute to the process of national reconciliation and to the restoration and maintenance of peace.'[26] In the following decades, criminal proceedings for the gravest atrocities have become a part of the broadened definition of peace.

The international legal order regards impunity as incompatible with peace and addresses this problem with a large number of mechanisms under conventional and customary law. The underlying foundation is the acknowledgment of the international community's responsibility and duty to enforce criminal prosecutions. As the President of the ICTR, Judge Erik Møse, observed:

> Over the span of a single decade, international criminal tribunals went from being a vague idea to an active reality, and have grown into institutions existing in their own rights. Henceforth, the international community's main concern should be to hold alleged perpetrators for human

---

committed by men, not by abstract entities and only by punishing individuals who commit such crimes can the provisions of international law be enforced.'

24 See, *e.g.* Cassese, *International Criminal Law*, p. 3.

25 ICC Preamble.

26 ICC Preamble.

rights abuses individually responsible for their actions. In cases where States are loath to punish such violations, or where they simply cannot do so, international tribunals are establishing practice and contribute to a culture of refusing impunity for human rights violations.[27]

The permanent international criminal court, the ICC, was created 'to put an end to impunity for the perpetrators of international crimes'.[28] The Preamble to the ICC Statute explicitly recognises the inherent relationship between peace and justice for core crimes, declaring that 'grave crimes threaten the peace, security, and wellbeing of the world' and marks the development from ad hoc post-conflict solutions to a permanent universal institution, creating a comprehensive and global criminal justice system.[29] Moreover, hybrid international prosecutions are set forward *inter alia* in the Special Court for Sierra Leone,[30] the Special Panel for Serious Crimes of the Dili District Court in East Timor,[31] and the Extraordinary Chambers of Cambodia.[32] Also, there is an increase in domestic prosecutions of international crimes, and third-state enforcement of universal jurisdiction.[33]

Despite these advances, numerous past atrocities have not been prosecuted.[34] In an overall perspective, prosecution of interna-

---

27 Erik Møse, cited in Francois-Xavier Nsanzuwera, in 'The ICTR Contribution to National Reconciliation', *Journal of International Criminal Justice*, 3 (4) (2005) pp. 944–49.

28 ICC Statute, Preamble.

29 Luis Moreno Ocampo, 'Chief Prosecutor of the International Criminal Court', in Ambos, Large, and Wierda (eds.), *Building a Future on Peace and Justice*, p. 10.

30 The Special Court for Sierra Leone was established on 16 January 2002 as a result of an agreement between the United Nations and the government of Sierra Leone, with jurisdiction over international crimes defined in the same manner as in the ICC Statute.

31 The East Timor Special Panels' entry into force on 6 June 2000.

32 The Extraordinary Chambers in the Courts of Cambodia established in an agreement between the UN and the Cambodian government in 2003 are formally part of the Cambodian judiciary, but can equally be seen as a mixed national/international tribunal. The courts will apply both international law and domestic law and operate in accordance with a Cambodian law of 2004.

33 See, *e.g.* Naomi Roht-Arriaza, 'The New Landscape of Transitional Justice' in N. Roht-Arriaza (ed.), *Transitional Justice in the Twenty-First Century: Beyond Truth versus Justice* (Cambridge University Press, 2006), p. 11.

34 See, *e.g.* 'Introduction', M. Cherif Bassouni (ed.), *Post-Conflict Justice* (Ardsley, NY: Transnational Publishers Inc., 2002).

tional crimes are rather the exceptions of justice. The post-conflict society's inability to deal with complex contextual elements and a large number of perpetrators often consigns justice to a 'luxury' they might not afford. Moreover, the current international prosecutions of the ICTY and ICTR are limited to the core international crimes and those persons in charge, and within the guarantees of a due process.[35] Furthermore, the ICTY and ICTR, due to their completion time schedules, budgetary difficulties and backlogs of cases, have turned to plea-bargaining to obtain guilty pleas, and to a rather controversial transfer of cases.[36] In addition, the hybrid courts of Sierra Leone and East Timor suffer from lack of funding and budgetary constraints. The ICC jurisdiction with its complementarity regime and the current choice of prosecutorial discretion is limited to a last resort court of those most responsible. The Court has very few enforcement mechanisms.[37]

Regardless of these problems, the normative pull of enforcing universal criminal prosecutions in order to combat impunity and the rejection of unconditional amnesties has created a valuable awareness in the international community to ensure that offenders of international crimes are brought to justice. Notwithstanding, domestic criminal proceedings remain crucial for the effective implementation of international criminal law.[38] Arguably, the goals of prosecutions on a domestic level regularly have a better chance of accomplishment if the affected society participates in these processes within its own legal culture. In this respect, restorative

---

35   For an illuminating elaboration of the prioritising criteria, see 'Observers' Notes'(Article by Article), by Morten Bergsmo and Pieter Kruger in Otto Triffterer (ed.), *Commentary on the Rome Statute of the International Criminal Court* (Munich: Beck, Hart, Nomos, 2008), Art. 53, 19f. and Office of the Prosecutor, *Policy Paper on the Interest of Justice*, September 2007.

36   Combs, *Guilty Pleas in International Criminal Law*, pp. 27–37.

37   ICC, *Prosecutor* v. *Lubanga Dyilo*, Decision concerning Pre-Trial Chamber I's Decision of 10 February 2006 and the Incorporation of Documents into the Record of the Case against Mr. Thomas Lubanga Dyilo, ICC-01/04-01706. 24 February 2006 at §§ 46-48. See also Office of the Prosecutor, *Report on Prosecutorial Strategy*, 14 September 2006.

38   For an elaboration see Markus Benzing, 'The Complementarity Regime of the International Criminal Court: International Criminal Justice between State Sovereignty and the Fight against Impunity,' in A. von Bogdandy and R. Wolfrum (eds.), *Max Planck Yearbook of United Nations Law*, Vol. 7, (Leiden: Koninklijke Brill N.V., 2003), pp. 591–632.

elements may operate as a key player to link traditional judicial measures with international standards. On the other hand, a recent empirical study of transitional societies shows that a majority prefer international criminal trials.[39]

6.2.3 *An absolute duty to prosecute? The scope of the states' obligations*

International law provides strong support for the principle that the most serious crimes of concern to the international community as a whole must be punished. The legal foundation for the determination of a concept of duty is the development of individual liability under international humanitarian law in the realm of the law of armed conflicts, particularly the grave breaches of the 1949 Geneva Conventions and the two additional protocols of 1977.[40] In addition, universal human rights conventions explicitly require prosecutions. According to the International Covenant on Civil and Political Rights (ICCPR), in the case of serious violations the states are obliged to prosecute, try and punish those responsible.[41] The Genocide Convention demands criminal prosecutions at both the international and domestic level.[42] The Convention against

39　Kiza, E., Rathgeber, C., and Rohne H.-C., *Victims of War: An Empirical Study on War-Victimization and Victims' Attitudes towards Addressing Atrocities* (Hamburg: Hamburger Institut für Sozialforschung, 2006) Hamburger edition online, available at http://www.his-online.de (last accessed 19 September 2010).

40　There are four Geneva Conventions. See First Geneva Convention for the Amelioration of the Condition of the Wounded and Sick in Armed Forces in the Field, 12 August 1949, Article 49; Second Geneva Convention for the Amelioration of the Conditions of Wounded, Sick and Shipwrecked Members of the Armed Forces, 12 August 1949, Article 50; Third Geneva Convention relative to the Treatment of Prisoners of War, 12 August 1949, Article 130; and Fourth Geneva Convention relative to the Treatment of Prisoners of War, 12 August 1949. See also the three additional protocols: Protocol I (1977): Protocol Additional relating to the Protection of Victims of International Armed Conflict; Protocol II (1977): Protocol Additional to the Geneva Conventions relating to the Protection of Victims of Non-International Armed Conflicts; Protocol III (2005) ... additional to the Geneva Conventions of 12 August 1949, and relating to the adoption of an Additional Distinctive Emblem. See most recently the sixth preamble paragraph of the 1998 ICC Statute.

41　Seibert-Fohr, *Prosecuting Serious Human Rights Violations*, p. 28.

42　Convention on the Prevention and Punishment of the Crime of Genocide, adopted 9 December 1948 by General Assembly Resolution 260 A (III) and entered into force 12 January 1951, 9 December 1948, 78 U.N.T.S. 227.

Torture obliges each state party to ensure that all acts of torture are offences under its criminal law.[43] Moreover, crimes against humanity are banned under customary law, as confirmed in the ICC Statutes Article 7.

The UN Security Council has affirmed the duty to prosecute: 'the responsibility of all States to put an end to impunity and to prosecute those responsible for genocide, crimes against humanity, and war crimes including those relating to sexual and other violence against women and girls and in this respect stresses the need to exclude these crimes, where feasible, from amnesty provisions'.[44] The Council in 2002 reaffirmed the responsibility to 'end impunity and prosecute the [persons] most responsible' for core crimes.[45] The scope of the states' obligations under international law to prosecute is confirmed by the UN Commission on Human Rights, in the Updated Principles.[46] According to Article 19:

> the state shall undertake prompt, thorough, independent and impartial investigations of violations of human rights law and international humanitarian law and take appropriate measures in respect of the perpetrators particularly in the area of criminal justice, by ensuring that those responsible for serious crimes under international law are prosecuted, tried and duly punished.

The premises underlying Article 19, which recognise that criminal prosecution plays a necessary role in combating impunity for serious crimes under international law, have been strongly affirmed in the jurisprudence and the practice of the human rights treaty bodies.

There is no conclusive evidence from current state practice that indicates whether the duty to prosecute breaches has reached

---

43 Convention against Torture and Other Cruel, Inhuman or Degrading Treatment or Punishment, offered the option of signature by General Assembly Resolution 39/46, U.N. General Assembly Official Records, 39th Session, Supplement No. 51 U.N. Doc. A/39/51, at p. 197, 4 February 1985 and entered into force 26 June 1987.

44 UN DOC, S/RES/1325/2000.

45 UN.DOC S/PRST/2002/41.

46 Updated Set of Principles for the Protection and Promotion of Human Rights through Actions to Combat Impunity, E/CN.4/2005/102/Add. 1, 8 February 2005.

the threshold of customary international law.[47] However, the ICRC study on customary law affirms the existence of a duty to prosecute.[48] Noticeably, the dissenting opinion of Judge AlKhasawheneh in the ICJ Arrest Warrant case presupposes a duty to prosecute *jus cogens*: 'The effective combating of grave crimes has arguably assumed a *jus cogens* character reflecting recognition by the international community of the vital community interest and values it seeks to protect and enhance. Therefore when hierarchically norms come into conflict with the rules of immunity, they should prevail.'[49] It is noteworthy that current schools of international law show a variety of solutions to the same scheme of interpretation. Some scholars, like Seibert-Fohr in her recent study of a duty to prosecute serious human rights violations, conclusively state that no customary law exists regarding a duty to prosecute outside the conventional law.[50] Others argue that the duty, based on an analysis of the jurisprudence of international courts and human rights bodies, has emerged to a *jus cogens* character.[51] However, an overly rigid model of an absolute duty appears inadequate to the desired bottom-up approach of post-conflict justice.

6.2.4 *The concept of reconciliation*

The post-conflict arguments for exemption from prosecution are usually accompanied by the concept of reconciliation as the core *raison d'être*. In order to assess whether a complementing restorative system may advance reconciliation, the meaning of the concept of reconciliation itself should be clarified. However, the concept may not easily bring about any obvious understanding. Furthermore, the necessary linkage to a restorative system falls short on empirical confirmation. Indeed, the reconciling power of criminal justice is not excluded from the concept of reconciliation.

---

47 Ambos, 'The Legal Framework of Transitional Justice', para. 8.
48 ICRC: Customary International Humanitarian Law 2005 at 607, rule 158.
49 ICJ Arrest Warrant, 2000 (*Democratic Republic of Congo* v. *Belgium*) 2002, ICJ REP. Separate opinion of Judge AlKhasawneh, para. 7.
50 Seibert-Fohr, *Prosecuting Serious Human Rights Violations*.
51 *E.g.* Alexander Orakhelashvili, *Peremptory Norms in International Law* (Oxford University Press, 2006).

In fact, in many cases prosecutions have been held as prerequisites for true reconciliation.[52]

Reconciliation, according to an definition given by Galtung, can be interpreted as 'the process of healing the traumas of both victims and perpetrators of violence providing a closure of the bad relation. The process prepares the parties for relations with justice and peace'.[53] However, the meaning of the concept of reconciliation is disputed, with different stakeholders groups holding differing interpretations as to its core substance, for instance by what measures reconciliation can be achieved, and its main objectives. Indeed, the term may be used to justify competing goals and competing positions, for instance between the position of former combatants and their victims. Lederach marks the dilemmas most expressively, noting that:

> reconciliation can be seen as dealing with three specific paradoxes. Firstly, in an overall sense, reconciliation promotes an encounter between the open expression of the painful past, on the one hand, and the search for the articulation of a long-term, interdependent future, on the other hand. Secondly, reconciliation provides a place for truth and mercy to meet, where concerns for exposing what has happened *and* for letting go in favour of renewed relationship are validated and embraced. Thirdly, reconciliation recognises the need to give time and place to both justice and peace, where redressing the wrong is held together with the envisioning of a common, connected future.[54]

Crocker describes the objectives of reconciliation, initially with the minimalist 'thin' conceptions like ceasefire and 'simple co-existence' between the warring parties. A 'thicker' conception of different levels of the society must allow for mutual respect and a deeper understanding, in the sense of 'social harmony' and 'forgiveness and mercy,' usually disseminated by a truth commission

---

52 See for instance the discussion in Erin Daly and Jeremy Sarkin, 'Too Many Questions, Too Few Answers. Reconciliation in Transitional Societies', *Columbia Human Rights Law Review*, 35 (2004), pp. 661–728.

53 Johan Galtung, in Mohammed Abu-Nimer (ed.), *Reconciliation, Justice and Co-existence in Theory and Practice* (Lanham, MD: Lexington Books, 2001).

54 John-Paul Lederach, *Building Peace: Sustainable Reconciliation in Divided Societies* (Washington, DC: United States Institute of Peace Press, 1997).

or community-based conflict resolutions.[55] Daly and Sarkin have elaborated these different levels on an individual, interpersonal, communal, national, and international basis.[56] Mallinder discusses whether the concepts of national unity, forgetting, forgiveness, and establishment of democracy will contribute to reconciliation, in the backdrop of 'the various ways in which states use the language of reconciliation to justify amnesty laws, often with very different outcomes'.[57] The reconciling effect of amnesty and forgiveness is then dependent on how these measures satisfy demands of a true reconciliation that have the ability to repair. Without acknowledgement and recognition of the past and the responsibility, such goals are not likely to be attained.[58]

In the African reconciliation concept of *ubuntu*, social harmony is the higher goal, which may prepare the ground for amnesty, e.g. the Truth and Reconciliation Commission (TRC) in South Africa: 'Amnesty per se cannot (...) have a reconciliatory effect and could in fact lead to the perpetuation of existing divisions, unless it is granted with due regard to certain requirements and principles.'[59]

---

55 David A Crocker, 'Reckoning with Past Wrongs: A Normative Framework', *Ethics & International Affairs*, 13 (1) (1999), pp. 43–64, and further developed in 'Punishment, Reconciliation and Democratic Deliberation', *Buffalo Criminal Law Review*, 5 (2) (2002), pp. 509–49. See also Mallinder, *Amnesty, Human Rights and Political Transition*, pp. 48–61.

56 Erin Daly and Jeremy Sarkin, *Reconciliation in Divided Societies: Finding Common Ground*, Pennsylvania Studies in Human Rights (Philadelphia: University of Pennsylvania Press, 2007).

57 Mallinder, *Amnesty, Human Rights and Political Transition*. She calls for a focal point not only on national reconciliation, but also for 'measures to encourage individual and communal reconciliation by talking neighbourhood disputes that are often overlooked in centrally organised programmes such as truth commissions.'

58 The use of 'false reconciliation' is introduced by Ignatieff, Méndez, and Lerche. These authors raise the alarm regarding placing the emphasis on truth, and sometimes, on the granting of an amnesty, as a clear misconception that 'truth' and denial of 'justice' always lead to reconciliation. Michael Ignatieff, 'Articles of Faith', *Index on Censorship*, 5 (1996), pp. 110–22; Juan E. Méndez, 'Accountability for Past Abuses', *Human Rights Quarterly*, 19 (2) (1997), pp. 255–82; and Charles Lerche, 'Peace Building Through Reconciliation', *The International Journal of Peace Studies*, 5 (2) (2000). On the same topic, Seibert-Fohr, *Prosecuting Serious Human Rights Violations*.

59 *Azanian Peoples Organization (AZAPO) v. The President of the Republic of South Africa* (CCT 17/96) BCLR 1915 (CC).

In the same mood, the Sierra Leone TRC acknowledged the amnesty in the Lomé Peace Accord 1999 which provided that 'the government shall (...) grant absolute and free pardon and reprieve to all combatants and collaborators in respect of anything done by them in pursuit of their objectives'. However, this amnesty was regarded as contradictory to international law; the statues of the Special Court of Sierra Leone (SCSL) Article 10 stated that: 'An amnesty (...) shall not bar prosecutions.'[60] In Uganda, the Amnesty Law of 2000 was considered 'a vital tool for reconciliation.' At the same time, the lack of a mechanism for truth telling or the admission of guilt on the part of former combatants hindered the process of reconciliation.[61]

6.2.5 Post-conflict exceptions

6.2.5.1 The peace versus justice dilemma

In post-conflict situations, the actors often argue that prosecutions of the crimes committed during the conflicts will threaten a fragile democracy, peace and reconciliation.[62] At the same time, the performance of criminal justice is essential for the victim's rights to truth, justice and reparation,[63] and re-establishment of the rule

---

60   See, *e.g.* for a further elaboration William A Schabas, 'Amnesty, the Sierra Leone Truth and Reconciliation Commission and the Special Court for Sierra Leone', *UC Davis Journal of International Law and Policy*, (2004), p. 145.

61   Refuge Law Project Working Paper No. 15, *Whose Justice? Perceptions of Uganda's Amnesty Act: The Potential for Conflict Resolution and Long-Term Reconciliation*, February 2005. See also E.K. Baines, 'The Haunting of Alice: Local Approaches to Justice and Reconciliation in Northern Uganda', *International Journal of Transitional Justice*, 1 (1) (2007), pp. 91–114. In a study conducted in 2005 by the International Center for Transitional Justice and The Human Rights Center (University of California, Berkeley), *Forgotten Voices – A Population-Based Survey on Attitudes about Peace and Justice in Northern Uganda*, a majority of the 2,585 respondents in Northern Uganda showed support for punishment by imposing trials (66 per cent). Only 18 per cent voted for an amnesty. Contrarily, in a study conducted by the Office of the High Commissioner for Human Rights (OHCHR) the people from Acholiland are, for pragmatic reasons, not in favour of prosecutions. OHCHR: *Making Peace Our Own: Victims' perceptions of Accountability and Transitional Justice in Northern Uganda*, 2007.

62   Gerhard Werle, *Principles of International Criminal Law* (The Hague: TMC Asser, 2005), p. 66.

63   ICC Statute Article 68 (3), 75.

of law.[64] The UN Secretary-General has addressed the dilemma as quoted: 'Justice and peace are not contradictory forces. Rather, properly pursued, they promote and sustain one another.'[65]

Criminal accountability for international crimes has indeed the potential for transforming societies emerging from repressive regimes and large-scale atrocities, reintroducing the rule of law and healing the wounds of the population, the moral issues and the national identity.[66] Moreover, as in domestic trials, significant aims of prosecutions can be achieved, such as retribution, deterrence, incapacitation and rehabilitation. However, the communicative function of prosecution is interdependent with other measures of reform and capacity building.[67] Trials are not magic formulas for social repair. The question of whether criminal punishment will serve peace and reconciliation drives a complex selection of legal criteria. Certainly, minimum standards like the universal protection against core crimes, the unconditional right to the truth, and the restriction to only good-faith complementing measures based on democratically adopted decisions, will rule out blanket unconditional amnesties.[68] Nevertheless, in several cases, the actors are left with the intricate balance between what procedures are instigated primarily to shield the perpetrators, and what measures are genuine in their attempts to combine the search for truth with the mechanism of social repair. Only the latter can justify an exception. Measures within this threshold are mostly truth commissions, operated by the state, which combine the search for truth and reconciliation with carefully crafted amnesties, in order to achieve societal restoration. The most famous and successful transition based on this formula is the South African TRC after the fall of the apartheid regime (see Section 6.4.2.2)

---

64 For a recent discussion, see Ellen Lutz and Caitlin Reiger, *Prosecuting Heads of State* (Cambridge University Press, 2009), p. 275.

65 UN Security Council, *The Rule of Law and Transitional Justice...*

66 See for instance Teitel, *Transitional Justice*, p. 67; A. Boraine, *A Country Unmasked: Inside South Africa's Truth and Reconciliation Commission* (Oxford University Press, 2001) pp. 280–81; Robinson, 'Serving the Interest of Justice', p. 489.

67 See Laurel E. Fletcher and Harvey M. Weinstein, 'Violence and Social Repair: Rethinking the Contribution of Justice to Reconciliation', *Human Rights Quarterly* (2002), pp. 573–639.

68 Ambos, 'The Legal Framework of Transitional Justice', at abstract, para. 2.

6.2.5.2 Towards a flexible approach?

Recent experience in the field of transitional justice shows that there cannot be a one-size-fits-all approach due to the variety of culture, religion, and national experiences.[69] A flexible approach is also supported in state practice.[70] Orentlicher confirms the cross-cultural perspective: 'Given the extraordinary range of national experiences and cultures, how could anyone imagine there to be a universally relevant formula for transitional justice?...The broader question of cultural relativism is, moreover, just as complex in respect of the perennial amnesty vs. prosecutions dilemma as in other contexts.'[71] In addition, the ICC Chief Prosecutor is aware of this delicate balance: 'In any Assessment of these efforts, the Office will take into consideration the need to respect the diversity of legal systems, traditions and cultures.'[72] However, as methodically elaborated by Ambos, the limitations *ratione materie* with regard to the international core crimes and the limitations *ratione personae* with regard to the persons most responsible, will limit the scope of a flexible approach.[73]

6.2.6 The anti-impunity paradigm and the contemporary terms of justice: Are they compatible?

Large-scale impunity for past abuses in post-conflict societies can still be found throughout the world, ranging from *de facto* inadequacies to the systematic granting of national amnesty laws. Often no complementing schemes have been carried out. Because of the nature of the crimes, usually mass crimes on a systematic level, the measures regarding justice are unavoidably related to the destiny of the state in transition. A society traumatised by war and ruined state structure, or a peace accord in favour of past abusers, will probably not make contributions to criminal justice. At the

69   UN Security Council, *The Rule of Law and Transitional Justice...*
70   Claus Kress and Lena Grover, 'International criminal law restraints in peace talks to end armed conflicts of a non-international character' in Morten Bergsmo and Pablo Kalmanovitz (eds.), *Law in Peace Negotiations*, FICHL Publication Series No. 5 (Peace Research Institute Oslo (PRIO), 2009), pp. 29–53.
71   Diane Orentlicher, 'Settling Accounts Revisited: Reconciling Global Norms with Local Agency', *The International Journal of Transitional Justice*, 1, (2007), pp. 10–22.
72   OTP, *Paper on some policy issues before the Office of the Prosecutor*, September 2003, p. 5.
73   Ambos, 'The Legal Framework of Transitional Justice', para. 21.

same time, as pointed out by Cassese, the international criminal landscape since the post-cold war's tribunals has been transformed dramatically: 'The certainty of impunity is gone.'[74] Indeed the international legal order against impunity for the most serious crimes and for the perpetrator most responsible itself proves a powerful antidote to impunity.[75] On the other hand, the term of justice in the post-conflict scenarios additionally encompasses a non-punitive element.

There are in particular four elements that affect the compatibility.

Firstly, as accounted for by the UN Secretary-General, prosecutions alone may not always serve a broadly construed idea of justice:

> Justice is an ideal of accountability and fairness in the protection and vindication of rights and the prevention and punishment of wrongs. Justice implies regard for the rights of the accused, for the interest of the victims and for the well-being of society. It is a concept rooted in all national cultures and traditions and, while its administration usually implies formal judicial mechanisms, traditional dispute resolution mechanisms are equally relevant.[76]

With this exceptionally broad definition, the Secretary-General has set a standard for the UN approach to post-conflict justice that inevitably includes elements of restorative justice. Arguably it should be read in conjunction with the prosecutorial discretion of the ICC Statute Article 53, and the competence to refrain from prosecution when 'not in the interests of justice'.

Secondly, measures regarding justice should serve the goals of human rights protection. Despite the enthusiasm for a global criminal justice system, prosecution is not an end in itself in the process of human protection. The overriding purpose is to ensure and secure human rights in accordance with peace and stability for the specific country, with the emphasis on what measures will best serve the transition.

Thirdly, the undertaking of prosecutions is regularly challenged in the post-conflict societies by insufficient resources, a

---

74 Cassese, *International Criminal Law*.
75 Orentlicher, 'Settling Accounts Revisited', p. 10.
76 UN Security Council, *The Rule of Law and Transitional Justice...*, para. 7.

dysfunctional judiciary and a high level of political disputation. Furthermore, impossibilities may follow from the fact that mass atrocities are often committed by state actors or with the complicity of the state. Accordingly, access to non-punitive mechanisms is regarded as a necessary means for societies emerging from repressive regimes. As stated by the UN Truth Commission for El Salvador in its report: 'Under certain conditions in a country there may be insurmountable difficulties in the prosecution of alleged perpetrators.'[77] The Commission advocated a future-orientated process of reconciliation and unification of society as 'a cardinal objective'.[78]

Fourthly, if justice presupposes reconciliation, restorative justice may offer a better option. In the case of South Africa, the TRC made the ambitious claim that to a larger degree than formal prosecutions, a restorative approach to past crimes could foster reconciliation. There are also current examples of a successful blend of retributive and restorative elements in internationalised criminal processes that synthesise various legal traditions into a coherent body of law and practice. In some of these cases, the trials for the gravest crimes are combined with truth commissions for a lower level of crimes, as in Sierra Leone, East Timor and Rwanda.

It is, however, not definite how these elements of an increased compatibility are advocated under the current jurisprudence of the international and regional legal institutions. Truth commissions that offer a historical record, public apology and forgiveness, may not after all fulfil the national duty to investigate and punish international crimes. The Human Rights Committee, ECHR and the Inter-American human rights institutions all apply strict requirements of investigation, prosecutions and punishment, and a rebuttable presumption against amnesties for serious violations.[79] Recent case law from ECHR advocates procedural obligations to secure

---

77   U.N. Commission for El Salvador, Report of the Commission on the Truth of El Salvador: From Madness to Hope, U.N: DOC S/25500, Annexes (1993). See also Thomas Buergenthal, 'The United Nations Truth Commission for El Salvador', *Vanderbilt Journal of Transnational Law*, 27 (3) (1994), 497.

78   *Ibid.*

79   See for instance the Barrios Altos case, Inter-American Court of Human Rights, 14 March 2001. For a comprehensive study of the duty to prosecute serious human rights violations, see Seibert-Fohr, *Prosecuting Serious Human Rights Violations*.

substantive rights capable of leading to the punishment of the offender through comprehensive criminalisation and the enforcement of it to secure human rights. Also in the domestic context, restorative justice to some degree is viewed as a form of accountability.[80] Interestingly, in the Justice and Peace Law Judgment of the Constitutional Court of Colombia, a balancing process based on proportionality was accepted as an instrument that passed the complementarity test under ICC statutes Article 17.[81] See Section 6.3.2 for a further discussion of the ICC.

6.3 A necessary instrument for restorative options: Admissibility of amnesties

6.3.1 General remarks

Blanket amnesty laws, which unconditionally block prosecution of gross violations of human rights, are generally recognised as incompatible with international standards. In the frequently cited decision on the Lomé Accord Amnesty in the Kallon case, the Special Court for Sierra Leone dismissed the ability of an amnesty to bind courts.[82] Moreover, the ICTY in the Furundzija verdict supported the existence of *jus cogens* norms and declared the prohi-

---

80 For instance in Northern Ireland, *e.g.* Bell, 'The New Law of Transitional Justice' in K. Ambos, J. Large, and M. Wierda (eds.), *Building a Future on Peace and Justice*, pp. 105–27, para. 2.5.

81 The Constitutional Court of Colombia in the Judgment of 18 May 2006 at § 4.2.2 on the Justice and Peace law found that a punishment or sanction must be proportional to the harm suffered. For a recent critical study on the Colombian Peace Law and the principle of complementarity of the ICC, see Kai Ambos, *The Colombian Peace Process and the Principle of Complementarity of the International Criminal Court: An Inductive, Situation-based Approach* (Berlin: Springer, 2010).

82 Decision on challenge to jurisdiction, Lomé Accord Amnesty in *Prosecutor v. Morris Kallon*, Brima Bazzy Kamara, SCSL-2004-15-PT-060-I, SCSL-2004-15-PT-060-II, Appeal (13.03.2004), para. 67. The United Nations attached a caveat to the Lomé Peace Accord in Sierra Leone, indicating that it did not consider the amnesty to apply to serious violations of international law. *Seventh Report of the Secretary-General on the United Nations Observer Mission in Sierra Leone*, Para. 7, UN SCOR, UN Doc S/1999/836/(1999) For a critique of the Court's decision see Sarah Williams, 'Amnesties in International Law: The Experience of the Special Court of Sierra Leone' *Human Rights Law Review*, 5 (2005) p. 271.

bition of torture as one of them, and, as such, an amnesty 'senseless to argue'.[83]

Throughout several resolutions and principles the UN has attempted to discourage impunity.[84] Amnesties, once uncontroversial for repressive rulers to negotiate as a pre-condition to the transfer of power, have been made difficult to enforce by the development of international law.[85] Notably, the Secretary-General has affirmed this conclusion: 'While recognizing that amnesty is an accepted legal concept and a gesture of peace and reconciliation at the end of a civil war or an internal armed conflict, the United Nations has consistently maintained the positions that amnesty cannot be granted in respect of international crimes, such as genocide, crimes against humanity or other serious violations of international humanitarian law.'[86]

On the other hand, the conditional amnesty may not be regarded as per se prohibited. The operation of the amnesty criteria runs parallel on how to decide whether a society has done everything possible to advance accountability, within a framework of democratic will. Robinson introduced a list of different criteria, generally recognised as relevant:

> Were the measures adopted by democratic will?
> Is the departure from the standards of criminal prosecutions of all offenders based on necessity, i.e. irresistible social, economic, or political realities?
> Is there a full and effective investigation into the facts?
> Does the fact-finding enquiry name names?
> Is the relevant commission or body independent and suitably resourced?
> Is there at least some form of punishment of perpetrators (are they identified, required to come forward, required to do community service, subject to lustration?
> Is some form of remedy or compensation provided to the victims?

---

83 *Prosecutor* v. *Furundzija*, No IT-95-17/1-T at 157-157 (10.12.1998).

84 See for instance The Joinet Report, E/CN.4/Sub 1997/20/Rev. 1, 2 October 1997, UN-ECOSOC Commission on Human rights, Promotion and Protection of Human Rights. Impunity, 27 February 2004, Princeton University Program in Law and Public Affairs, The Princeton Principles on Universal Jurisdiction 28 (2001).

85 Paul van Zyl and Mark Freeman, 'Conference Report' in Alice H. Henkin (ed.), *The Legacy of Abuse*.

86 UN Secretary General UNDOC 5/2000/915, (4 October 2000).

Does the national approach provide a sense of closure or justice to victims? Is there a commitment to comply with other human rights obligations?[87]

These questions will be especially useful as an autonomous and democratically based evaluation on the legitimacy of the measures.[88] They are also highly applicable to the use of restorative elements.

6.3.2 The ICC and amnesties

The controversial question the Court still has not resolved is whether a national decision to grant amnesty on the condition of disclosure of the truth before a judicial or quasi-judicial body in general reflects a purpose to shield the person concerned from criminal responsibility and therefore a genuine unwillingness of the state to prosecute. The alternative view is that the conduct serves a greater objective, based on the circumstances and exigencies of the situation.[89] Whether conditional amnesties on the conditions of full disclosure of the truth before a judicial or quasi-judicial body should be regarded as the latter, is disputed to a remarkable extent and calls for a narrow interpretation.[90] The exception for truth commissions will most probably be interpreted strictly, but a South African style of conditional amnesty for political crimes is not necessarily disadvantageous to accountability.

87 Robinson, 'Serving the Interest of Justice'.
88 See also Carsten Stahn, 'Complementarity, Amnesties and Alternative Forms of Justice: Some Interpretative Guidelines for the International Criminal Court', *Journal of International Criminal Justice*, 3 (2005).
89 Anja Seibert-Fohr, 'The Relevance of the Rome Statutes of the International Criminal Court for Amnesties and Truth Commissions', in A. von Bogdandy and R. Wolfrum (eds.), *Max Planck Yearbook of United Nations Law*, pp. 553–90, Andreas O'Shea, *Amnesty for Crimes in International Law and Practice* (The Hague: Kluwer, 2002), pp. 332–36.
90 For those arguing in favour of Rome Statute Article 17(1)(b) as the only applicable rule on a state's decision not to investigate or prosecute: *e.g.* Ambos, 'The Legal Framework of Transitional Justice', p. 46; Robinson, 'Serving the Interest of Justice', p. 499; Seibert-Fohr, 'The Relevance of the Rome Statutes...', pp. 567–76; Stahn, 'Complementarity, Amnesties and Alternative Forms of Justice'; for deviating views: O'Shea, *Amnesty for Crimes in International Law and Practice*, p. 126; and John Dugard, 'Possible Conflicts of Jurisdiction with Truth Commissions', in Antonio Cassese, Paola Gaeta and John R.W.D. Jones (eds.), *The Rome Statue of the International Criminal Court* (Oxford University Press, 2002), p. 698.

The ICC Statute seems at first sight to outlaw amnesties regarding the crimes otherwise falling within the jurisdiction of the Court. The Preamble states that the most serious crimes of concern to the international community as a whole 'must not go unpunished'. Effective prosecution must be ensured by taking measures at the national level and by enhancing international co-operation and thus contributing to the prevention of such crimes. The Preamble recalls that it is 'the duty of every state to exercise jurisdiction over those responsible for international crimes'.[91] At the preparatory conference for the ICC however, the US delegation suggested that amnesties in the interest of international peace and national reconciliation should be taken into account when deciding on jurisdiction, balancing the need to 'close a door to the conflict of the past era'.[92] Fear of endangering the South African TRC was a crucial part of the context.[93] Thus, the closer determination was 'deliberately evaded'.[94]

Accordingly, the ICC Statute contains no explicit rule dealing with the issues of national amnesties or equivalent national decisions of non-prosecutions.[95] In fact, the question is left open for the Court to solve, leaving the ICC Statutes Article 17 and 53 as flexible instruments. Blanket amnesties will generally not pass the

---

91 ICC Preamble.
92 *Cf.* O'Shea proposed an amendment to the ICC statutes to modify jurisdiction of the Court in order to allow for amnesties under certain circumstances. O'Shea, *Amnesty for Crimes in International Law and Practice*, pp. 332–36. These views are opposed by Seibert-Fohr in *Prosecuting Serious Human Rights Violations* (p. 286) who argues: 'it is questionable whether such an abstract agreement could give adequate guidance and would ultimately serve the protection of human rights.'
93 Kofi Annan, cited in Charles Villa-Vicencio, 'Why Perpetrators Should Not Always be Prosecuted: Where the International Criminal Court and Truth Commissions Meet', *Emory Law Journal*, 49 (2000).
94 Ambos, 'The Legal Framework of Transitional Justice', p. 69.
95 *E.g.* John R. Bolton, 'The Risks and Weaknesses of the International Criminal Court', *Law and Contemporary Problems*, 64 (2001) p. 178. The US delegation circulated a NON-Paper on the issue of State Practice regarding amnesties and pardon, see US Delegation, Draft paper, ICC PrepCom, 17 August 1997, which gives a summary of some of the most significant amnesties enacted and pardons granted prior to the establishment of the ICC. For further discussion, see Jessica Gavron, 'Amnesties in the Light of Development of International Law and the Establishment of the International Criminal Court', *International and Comparative Law Quarterly*, 51 (2002), pp. 93–95.

'complementarity test' under Article 17 (1) b. Conditional amnesties coupled with non-judicial measures, adopted in good faith in respect of traditional forms of justice, may be accepted, also if no criminal investigation has taken place.[96] However, the state may, independently, be regarded as unwilling if the main intention is to shield the perpetrators from prosecutions. The examination is, according to Ambos, 'essentially normative focusing on the quality of the proceedings and intimately linked to this – the unwillingness and inability of the domestic system concerned'.[97]

Article 17 is of a rather technical nature, while Article 53 creates extra room for manoeuvre for prosecutorial discretion. Even if a case has passed the admissibility test of Article 17, Article 53 of the ICC Statute permits the ICC prosecutor not to prosecute when the prosecutor concludes that there are 'substantial reasons to believe that an investigation would not serve the interests of justice'. The term justice interpreted broadly connotes that the prosecutor may as a part of the 'substantial reasons' consider the effect of complementing measures of a restorative nature.[98] Conclusively, the text of the ICC Statute does not justify amnesty as such, but the regime remains under certain extraordinary circumstances available to the peace mediators.[99]

PART II: RESTORATIVE JUSTICE AS A
COMPLEMENT TO PROSECUTIONS

6.4 The advantages of restorative justice in post-conflict societies

6.4.1 General remarks

The individual poses the right to forgive, whereas the choice of punishment rests in the society's interest. Restorative justice asks

96 See the wording of Article 17 (1) (a): 'being investigated', which includes non-judicial forms of investigations.
97 Ambos, 'The Legal Framework of Transitional Justice'.
98 *Ibid.*
99 *E.g.* Michael Sharf, 'The Amnesty Exception to the Jurisdiction of the International Criminal Court', *Cornell International Law Journal*, 32 (1999), p. 507.

for other responses to criminal justice than the determination of guilt and imprisonment. The restorative element provides for measures that will satisfy political, moral and normative standards, justified in a narrative of a relationship between accountability and reconciliation. Whilst retributive systems focus on the crime and the appropriate punishment, restorative approaches emphasise the need to repair relationships. Restorative justice is not only backward-looking, addressing the past crimes, but also forward-looking as it seeks to establish a more harmonious society.[100] Punishment then is not the objective.

In a post-conflict society a restorative justice process recognises that crimes have affected the society as a whole. The process will attempt to recognise the humanity of the opponents by addressing the faults of one's own community. Minow describes the aim of restorative justice in the fields of international law as: 'To repair the injustice, to make up for it, and to effect corrective changes in record, in relationships and in the future behavior'.[101] Mani introduces as a complementary term to restorative justice the phase reparative justice similar to 'signing a social contract'.[102]

A skilful combination of retributive and restorative elements may contribute to a process that guarantees the victims participation and gives the society legal tools to achieve goals that are beyond retribution. Restorative justice involves a shift in attention away from the mainly punitive judicial system and gives the state ownership of the problem of crime and its solutions. Consequently, restorative justice can be used to reduce the burden on the criminal justice system, to take cases out of the system elsewhere, and to provide a variety of constructive sanctions. For these reasons, restorative justice is increasingly accommodated within the states' justice systems and promoted by the United Nations.

100 See generally Guillermo Kerber, 'Overcoming Violence and Pursuing Justice: An Introduction to Restorative Justice Procedures', *The Ecumenical Review*, 55 (2), (April 2003), pp. 151–57; Dennis Sullivan and Larry Tiffs (eds.), *Handbook for Restorative Justice: A Global Perspective* (London: Routledge, 2006).

101 Martha Minow, *Between Vengeance and Forgiveness: Facing History after Genocide and Mass Violence* (Boston: Beacon Press, 1998), p. 104.

102 Rama Mani, 'Reparation as a Component of Transitional Justice in the Aftermath of a Violent Conflict: Pursuing "Reparative Justice" in the Aftermath of Violent Conflicts' in K. de Feyter, S. Parmentier et al. (eds.), *Out of the Ashes* (Antwerp: Intersentia, 2005), pp. 53–82.

Restorative justice can be especially appropriate where retributive justice influenced by the West is impossible due to practical and political conditions, or when restorative mechanisms may be the preferred approach to justice due to the legal culture, which is the case in many African societies. The traditional concept of *ubuntu* in South Africa, which roughly translated means 'humaneness and largeness of spirit', the *Gacaca* in Rwanda and the Acholi rites *(mato oput)* in Uganda are partly non-punitive in their character. In the choice of whether to punish or pardon, the concept of the African models aims to encourage an integration of the offender back into the community.

6.4.2 Truth commissions as the main instrument

6.4.2.1 General remarks

According to the Updated Set of Principles, the society has the right to know the truth about past events:

> Every people has the inalienable right to know the truth about past events concerning the perpetration of heinous crimes and about the circumstances and reasons that led, through massive or systematic violations, to the perpetration of those crimes. Full and effective exercise of the right to the truth provides a vital safeguard against the recurrence of violations.[103]

More than thirty truth commissions have been established during the past few decades. More recent truth commissions have generally been considered to constitute serious efforts to investigate and publicise the truth.[104] According to the authoritative definition from the UN Secretary-General:

---

103 UN Commission for Human Rights, 'Updated Set of Principles for the Protection and Promotion of Human Rights through Action to Combat Impunity', 8 February 2005, UN Doc E/CN.4/2005/102/Add1 (prepared by Diane Orentlicher).

104 Martha Minow, *Between Vengeance and Forgiveness*, pp. 59–60: 'Truth commissions undertake to write the history of what happened as a central task. For judges at trial, such histories are the by-product of particular moments of examining and cross-examining witnesses and reviewing evidence about the responsibility of particular individuals.'

Truth commissions are official, temporary, non-judicial fact-finding bodies that investigate a pattern of abuses of human rights or humanitarian law committed over a number of years. These bodies take a victim-centered approach and conclude their work with a final report of findings of fact and recommendations. (...) Truth commissions have the potential to be of great benefit in helping post-conflict societies establish the facts about past human rights violations, foster accountability, preserve evidence, identify perpetrators and recommend reparations and institutional reforms. They can also provide a public platform for victims to address the nation directly with their personal stories and can facilitate public debate about how to come to terms with the past. (...) Truth commissions are invariably compromised if appointed through a rushed or politicised process. They are best formed through consultative processes that incorporate public views on their mandates and on commissioner selection. To be successful, they must enjoy meaningful independence and have credible commissioner selection criteria and processes. Strong public information and communication strategies are essential to manage public and victim expectations and to advance credibility and transparency. Their gender sensitivity and responsiveness to victims and to victims of discrimination must be assured. Finally, many such commissions will require strong international support to function, as well as respect by international partners for their operational independence.[105]

Victim-centred face-to-face confrontations between the victims and the perpetrators provide a historical account of the period under question.[106] The work of respected truth commissions can facilitate a more complex understanding of underlying premises for mass atrocities and advance a process of social inclusion by engaging the society in a comprehensive process of repair. Trials alone, when operating in a remote distance from the public, and beyond the legal culture of the country where the atrocities occurred,

---

105 UN Security Council, *The Rule of Law and Transitional Justice...*, para. 50.
106 For a comprehensive analysis see generally: Priscilla B. Hayner, *Unspeakable Truths: Facing the Challenge of Truth Commissions* (New York: Routledge, 2002). Hayner documents twenty-one truth commissions in her definitive work on the subject: these truth commissions investigated atrocities in Argentina, Bolivia, Burundi, Chad, Chile, Ecuador, El Salvador, Germany, Guatemala, Haiti, Nepal, Nigeria, Sierra Leone, South Africa, Sri Lanka, Uganda, Uruguay and Zimbabwe. See also recently Hayner, 'Truth Commissions: A Schematic Overview', *International Review of the Red Cross*, 88 (862), (2006), pp. 295–310.

may not constitute the crucial pillar to the political context of the crimes.

For a truth commission's offer of amnesty in exchange for truth to be an adequate alternative to international norms, the commission should at least be a separate institution created formally by law, rather than established through executive policy. Secondly, the truth commission should pursue a restorative conception of justice that involves revealing the truth, repairing the harm to victims and promoting reconciliation.[107] It should accommodate all those affected by the conflict: offenders, victims and the wider community.[108]

Whether a truth commission as an alternative to prosecutions will satisfy the requirement of a criminal justice system inter alia under the ECHR and the ICC has not yet been decided. The purpose of such an inquiry is to foster reconciliation and bring to light the truth of the alleged offences, in exchange for the granting of amnesties and thus contrary to prosecutions. The ECHR has under current jurisprudence strongly emphasised the victims' rights to an investigation capable of leading to criminal justice. In this respect, it is unclear whether an investigation from a truth commission can satisfy these requirements.[109]

6.4.2.2 The TRC in South Africa: The ideal?

The truth commission that is most clearly associated with the principles of restorative justice is the South African TRC.[110] The Truth and Reconciliation Commission established in South Africa following the end of apartheid focused on reconciliation, heal-

---

107 Declan Roche, 'Truth Commission Amnesties and the International Criminal Court', *British Journal of Criminology*, 45 (2005), pp. 565 and 596.

108 For a broad-based recommendation list on truth commissions, see, *e.g.* Ambos, 'The Legal Framework of Transitional Justice', para. 16.

109 ECHR has established some criteria for a body of truth commission to be accepted. ECHR, *Hugh Jordan v. UK* (4 May 2001) Judgment 24746/94 (2001) ECHR 327, para. 11. See Seibert-Fohr, *Prosecuting Serious Human Rights Violations*.

110 For comprehensive analysis on the TRC see Jeremy Sarkin, *Carrots and Sticks: The TRC and the South African Amnesty Process* (Antwerp: Intersentia, 2004); Jennifer J. Llewellyn and Robert Howse, 'Institutions for Restorative Justice: The South African Truth and Reconciliation Commission', *University of Toronto Law Journal*, 49 (3) (1999), p. 355; Desmond Tutu, *No Future without Forgiveness* (London: Rider, 1999), pp. 107 f., and recently, 'Reflections on Moral Accountability', *International Journal of Transitional Justice*, 1 (1) (2007), pp. 6–7.

ing and forgiveness. Based on the Promotion of National Unity and Reconciliation Act, the TRC comprised three divisions: the Committee on Human Rights Violations, to hear the testimony of the victims; the Committee on Amnesty, to decide whether to grant an amnesty to individual applications; and the Committee of Reparation and Rehabilitation, to recommend measures to the government. Amnesty should be offered for acts 'associated with a political objective'. The TRC offered freedom from all punishment, criminal or civil, in exchange for full disclosure of the political crimes, based on the belief that amnesty would encourage the perpetrators to reveal the truth.

The commission was granted wide powers to arrest suspects and operated an advanced scheme of witness protection. The hearings were public. The Government conducted a few high-profile trials for apartheid offences. The TRC received more than 7,000 amnesty applications, mostly from low-level offenders. Of these, 1,167 were offered amnesty. A majority were rejected, because they related to ordinary offences.

The TRC contained several elements of restorative justice. It used a face-to-face confrontation between the victims and their offenders and permitted victims to cross-examine the amnesty applicants. It held public hearings to illuminate the roles of various actors in civil society in supporting and perpetrating apartheid. The offenders were encouraged to acknowledge their offences, face-to-face with the victims.

The process has been criticised, however, for having no limitations for the core crimes.[111] Markedly, the South African Constitutional Court in the AZAPO case stated that amnesties affect fundamental rights and might conflict with the right to judicial guarantees, but in the end chose to leave the choice of prosecution to the legislators facing the political realities:

> If the Constitution kept alive the prospect of continuous retaliation
> and revenge, the agreement of those threatened by its implementation
> might never have been forthcoming, and if it had, the bridge itself would
> have remained wobbly and insecure, threatened by fear from some and
> anger from others. It was for this reason that those who negotiated the

111 See Sarkin, note 264.

Constitution made a deliberate choice, preferring understanding over vengeance, reparation over retaliation, *ubuntu* over victimalisation'.[112]

None the less, a major and continuing concern is that those persons who did not fulfil the conditions of an amnesty have not been systematically prosecuted. This situation could certainly undermine the whole rationale of the TRC.

PART III: RWANDA AND AFGHANISTAN: THE PATHWAY TO A BIFURCATED PROCESS

6.5 Rwanda and the Gacaca courts

In Rwanda the use of elements of informal justice system from the local Gacaca has complemented the international prosecutions of the genocide in the ICTR and national courts, in a blend of retributive and restorative elements.

In 1994 a large-scale genocide took place in Rwanda.[113] The Rwandan population is composed of two major groups, the Hutus and the Tutsis. Over a period of 100 days Rwandan Hutus massacred approximately eight hundred thousand Rwandans, mostly Tutsis but also moderate Hutus. The killings ended when the Rwandan Patriotic Front (RPF) defeated the Rwandan army in July 1994. The international community made modest efforts to stop the massacres. A UN peacekeeping force stationed in Rwanda when the killings started was reduced by the Security Council from 1515 to 270. In May 1994, the UN Commission on Human Rights issued a report stating that 'the authors of the atrocities ...cannot escape personal responsibility for criminal acts carried out, ordered or condoned'. The Security Council established a commission of experts, similar to the one it had established for the former Yugoslavia. Finally the Security Council adopted Resolution 955

---

112 *Azanian Peoples Organization (AZAPO)* v. *The President of the Republic of South Africa* (CCT 17/96) BCLR 1915 (CC). For an overview of this case, see Sarkin, *Carrots and Sticks*.

113 For comprehensive literature of the Rwandan genocide, see Allison Des Forges, *Leave None to Tell the Story: Genocide in Rwanda* (New York: Human Rights Watch, 1999).

providing for the creation of the ICTR for the trials of those who had been most responsible.[114]

The Tutsi-led Rwandan government embarked on a large-scale national criminal prosecution. By 1998, roughly 130,000 people had been arrested on genocide charges. Rwanda adopted laws classifying the offenders into four categories depending on their level of culpability.[115] Because of the estimate that it would take more than two hundred years to try all prisoners by ordinary trials, the Rwandan government decided to transform a pre-colonial community-based system of dispute resolution known as Gacaca into a managed system for trying genocide cases. The Gacaca was originally used to resolve low-level disputes, typically property rights, matrimonial disputes and legacy questions. In 2001 the Rwandan government adopted a law that in a general way led to the establishment of eleven thousand Gacaca jurisdictions in small communities empowered to administer categories 2 and 3 crimes.

The courts' jurisdiction encompasses the authority to impose criminal sanctions, and to enhance truth-telling and reconciliation through the use of a guilty plea procedure. The conditions are that the accused makes a full and complete confession and apology, and reveals the locations of his/her victims. The courts are informally structured, operated by inhabitants of the local area, and require face-to-face confrontations and exposure of the harm perpetrated on victims.[116] Conclusively, the Gacaca courts offer a unique blend of retributive and restorative elements.[117]

---

114 L.J. van den Herik, *The Contribution of the Rwanda Tribunal to the Development of International Law* (Leiden: Martinus Nijhoff Publishers, 2005), pp. 27–84.

115 Organic Law No. 08/96. For a case study, see Mallinder, *Amnesty, Human Rights and Political Transition*, p. 107.

116 For further reading, see Allison Corey and Sandra F. Joireman, 'Retributive Justice: The Gacaca Courts in Rwanda', *African Affairs*, 103 (2004), pp. 73–89; William A. Schabas, 'Genocide Trials and *Gacaca* Courts', *Journal of International Criminal Justice*, 3 (2005), pp. 879–95.

117 For further reading, Jessica Harper, 'The Gacaca Experiment: Rwanda's Restorative Dispute Resolution Response to the 1994 Genocide,' *Pepperdine Dispute Resolution Law Journal*, 1 (2005); Coel Kirkby, 'Rwanda's *Gacaca* Courts: A Preliminary Critique', *Journal of African Law*, 50 (2), (2006), pp. 94–117; Erin Daly, 'Between Punitive and Restorative Justice: The Gacaca Courts in Rwanda', *Journal of International Law and Politics*, 34 (2002), p. 355; Mark A Drumbl, 'Law and Atrocity: Settling Accounts in Rwanda', *Ohio Northern University Law Review* 31 (2005), p. 41.

6.6 Stalemate in Afghanistan

6.6.1 Introduction

In Afghanistan, after just over thirty years of warfare and civil strife, the population is faced with blatant impunity for all levels of offenders.[118] The section will discuss this stuck position and its origin. Afghanistan joined the United Nations in 1946 and was party to almost a full scope of the conventions of humanitarian law and human rights law.[119] Consequently the essential framework of the duty to prosecute is applicable. Additionally, Afghanistan has ratified the ICC Statute in 2003. The legal toolbox for accountability measures in the peace process is conclusively available. The case of Afghanistan in this respect may be seen as a litmus test of whether criminal justice under the normative schemes of international law pertains to a universal legal regime.[120]

The state-building process, launched in the UN-brokered Bonn Agreement from 2001[121] after the ousting of the Taliban regime,

---

118 The assessment of the justice sector and rule of law from 2007, chaired by M. Cherif Bassiouni, concluded on the issue of transitional justice: 'Following decades of brutal conflicts that produced the death of hundreds of thousands of Afghans[, many] of whom were civilians, the mass displacement of millions and extraordinary suffering, there is a pressing need for engaging with the violence [of] the past. Accountability for past human rights violations is of great significance for the Afghan people. These processes should be developed in close consultation with the Afghan people and must integrate both Islamic law and Afghan cultural traditions. With this in mind it is likely that religious and tribal leaders will play a substantial role on any effective traditional justice program for Afghanistan, especially as regards advances in local communities.' *An Assessment of the Justice Sector and Rule of Law Reform in Afghanistan and the Need for a Comprehensive Plan*. Paper prepared for the Rome Conference, 'The Rule of Law in Afghanistan,' 2–3 July 2007.

119 Afghanistan has *inter alia* ratified the four 1999 Geneva Conventions, the 1977 Additional Protocols, the Genocide convention, the Torture Convention, ICCPR, CEDAR and the Rome Statutes.

120 Center for Economic and Social Rights (CESR) Report, *Human Rights and Reconstruction in Afghanistan* (New York: CESR, 2002), pp. 1–2: 'At stake is not only the ability of the Afghans to enjoy their fundamental rights but the very legitimacy of the United Nations as the unbiased guardian of international law and guarantor of peace and security for all peoples in the world.'

121 Agreement on Provisional Arrangements in Afghanistan Pending the Re-establishment of Permanent Government Institutions, also known as the Bonn Agreement after the location of its signature. Doc.s/2001/1154 of 5 December 2001.

has been slow and inefficient in the shadow of the ongoing war on terror. The Bonn Agreement provides an admirable framework of interim constitutional mechanisms for the transition to peace and democracy and institutional designs, but fails to provide any accountability measures on past abuses. International law as exercised indeed turned down the 'hard law' of several treaties and conventions on individual criminal liability in the cases of international crime. The stakeholders of the Afghan peace process, both the domestic parties and the international actors, adjudicated a 'peace first, justice later' policy from the very outset. It is widely agreed that this event of non-intervention of justice mechanisms contributed to widespread impunity in Afghanistan. At the present time this remains a major obstacle to reinstating the rule of law and consequently threatens the legitimacy of a continuous foreign intervention.[122]

There is currently a division between the population's quest for accountability and legal institutions to enforce such mechanisms.[123] Afghanistan's justice reforms since the 2001 invasion have suffered under rather unsuccessful experiments of importing Western traditions of positive law and legal institutions.[124] The justice reform had failed to link reforms to 'the foundation for justice in Afghanistan'.[125] The traditional and informal dispute mechanisms based on customary law, the *jirgas* and *shuras*[126] may serve as a tool for the implementation of transitional justice measures.[127] The Human Development Report for Afghanistan for 2007 made a principal recommendation to build on the informal justice sys-

---

122 Barnett Rubin, 'Transitional Justice and Human Rights in Afghanistan', *International Affairs*, 79 (3) (2003), pp. 567–81.

123 See Astri Suhrke and Kaja Borchgrevink, 'Negotiating Justice Sector Reform in Afghanistan', *Crime, Law and Social Change*, 51 (2) (2009), pp. 211–30.

124 For a critical analysis see Shahrbanou Tadjbakhsh and Michael Schoiswohl, 'Playing with Fire? The International Community's Democratization Experiment in Afghanistan', *International Peacekeeping*, 15 (2) (2008), pp. 252–67.

125 M. Cherif Bassiouni et al., *An Assessment of the Justice Sector...*, p. 35.

126 *Jirga* would mean the gathering of a small/large number of the Pashto tribal society, operating the dictates of pashtunwali. *Shura* is the *Dari* word for *jirga*. For further elaboration, see A. Wardak, 'Jirga: Power and Traditional Conflict Resolution in Afghanistan', in John Strawson (ed.), *Law after Ground Zero* (London: Routledge Cavendish, 2002), pp. 187–204.

127 *Peace, Reconciliation and Justice in Afghanistan*, Action Plan of the Government of the Islamic Republic of Afghanistan, 6–7 June 2005.

tem.[128] On the other hand, the Afghan population in a national consultation in 2005 was overwhelmingly in favour of criminal trials of the leaders most responsible.[129] These findings were upheld in recent empirical research, which shows that a majority prefer such trials to take place before an international court.[130]

The international community has on many occasions proved a catalyst and enforcer in the fields of international criminal law. In the case of Afghanistan, the war on terror may have influenced an incoherent enforcement of the international public order.[131] The current position offers neither retribution nor restoration, in a climate of ongoing conflict. This gives rise to several intriguing questions as a backdrop to the discussion: (1) Is security still the most fundamental factor? (2) Are retribution and restoration so closely linked that they are more likely to appear together than separated? (3) Does the stalemate substantiate the theory that retribution and restoration are compatible complements and not substitutes?

The reshape of a rule of impunity to the rule of law is then, accordingly, not a national matter but a determination of the international legal order, which indeed the Afghans should not be left to manage alone. As stated by Maley: 'Restoration of the rule of law is thus not just an abstract ideal; it is an essential component of any meaningful strategy to legitimate the new Afghan state and the post-Taliban order more broadly.'[132] The UN-endorsed Bonn Agreement did make some references to the idea of reconciliation. In the fourth paragraph of the Bonn Agreement the parties reaffirm the participants' determination to 'end the tragic conflict in Afghanistan and promote national reconciliation, lasting peace,

---

128 Afghan Human Development Report 2007, *Bridging Modernity and Tradition: Rule of Law and the Search for Justice*, pp. 95–96.

129 The Afghan Independent Human Rights Commission, *A Call for Justice* (Kabul: AIHRC, 2005).

130 Kiza, Rathgeber and Rohne, *Victims of War*.

131 For a discussion of the inconsistency of the Security Council Resolutions, see Gilles Dorronsoro, 'The Security Council and the Afghan Conflict', in V. Lowe, A. Roberts, J. Welsh and D. Zaum (eds.), *The United Nations Security Council and War: The Evolution of Thought and Practice since 1945* (Oxford University Press, 2008), pp. 446f.

132 William Maley, *The Afghanistan Wars*, 2nd edition (London: Palgrave Macmillan, 2009).

stability, and respect for human rights'.[133] Both the Afghan leaders and the international parties emphasised the Bonn process as a transition from a conflict to a new era of peace. No less importantly, the international actors symbolised themselves as peace-builders, in a UN-endorsed stabilisation mission of the post-conflict Afghanistan.

6.6.2 National consultations

The Afghan communities live with the memories and effects of grave human rights violations, including large-scale illegal arrests and abductions, murder, torture, summary executions, mass rapes, massacres, and random bombings. According to a nationwide survey conducted by the Afghanistan Independent Human Rights Commission (AIHRC) in 2005, 69 per cent of the Afghans consulted perceived that they or their family members had suffered serious human rights violations during the years of conflict, and 76 per cent thought that accountability through criminal proceedings would positively affect the security situation by increasing stability.[134] However, reconciliation as a concept of restoring relationships has a certain resonance for the Afghans. Although 66 per cent of the respondents found that criminal justice constitutes a major factor in the perceptions of justice, there was some support for reconciliatory mechanisms, if the process would focus on the leaders and commanders who were the architects of the conflicts, as being not yet reconciled. Twenty-six per cent indicated that such a reconciliation process could be advanced by the inclusion of traditional dispute mechanisms, such as *jirga* and *shura*. Ninety-five per cent agreed that truth-seeking was an important factor, but virtually none had any knowledge of the workings of a truth

133 Agreement on Provisional Arrangements in Afghanistan Pending the Reestablishment of Permanent Government Institutions, also known as the Bonn Agreement after the location of its signature. Doc.s/2001/1154 of 5 December 2001.

134 See Afghan Independent Human Rights Commission, *A Call for Justice: A National Consultation on Past Human Rights Violations* (Kabul: AIHRC, 29 January 2005). During a period of eight months, 4,151 respondents took part in the quantitative survey. In addition, 200 focus groups were convened including over 2,000 participants constituting the in-depth qualitative part of the study. Thirty-two out of 34 Afghan provinces were included.

commission.[135] However, as argued by Semple: 'Given the long and rich tradition of duplicity in counterinsurgency and Afghan warfare, there is a significant gray area of actions that protagonists may present as reconciliation, but that are actually tactical moves calculated to gain advantage.'[136]

6.6.3 Post-Bonn impunity

6.6.3.1 Introduction
Many of those now in positions of power or influence are widely held to be responsible for past crimes. In a country marked by the barefaced power of warlords, foreign occupation and a collapse of legal institutions, the norm of justice is postponed for an indefinite term. Astoundingly few in the international community have raised their voice to demand the establishment of an international trial, a truth commission or to claim a nullification of the 2009 Afghan amnesty law for war crimes. The rule-of-law institutions have been either completely destroyed or severely damaged by high-level corruption. There are, however, some significant steps towards reconciliation that at least on a formal basis indicate a growing awareness. Nevertheless, so far they have all failed to make a substantial difference.

The post-Bonn period has been marked by the increasing insurgency that was already appearing in 2003, and has accelerated ever since. In these phases, the goals of reconciliation have changed, from the original idea of post-conflict reconciliation after the fighting had ended, to the current attempts to stabilise a worsening insurgency, in fact a war, in which the international actors also take full part.

6.6.3.2 The Amnesty Law
The controversial Amnesty, National Reconciliation and Stability Law (hereinafter the Amnesty Law) entered into force with its

---

135 *Ibid.*
136 For an overview of pre-Bonn reconciliation processes, see Michael Semple, *Reconciliation in Afghanistan* (Washington, DC: United States Institute of Peace Press, 2009), pp. 13–35. See also Matt Walden, *Community Peacebuilding in Afghanistan* (Oxford: OXFAM International, 2008).

publication in December 2009 in the 'Official Gazette' No. 965.[137] The scope of the amnesty according to definitions under legal doctrine entails a *non-conditional blanket* amnesty that does not require any application or initial inquiry.[138] Because it is passed by the government to shield state agents, it is also a *self-amnesty*.[139] Article 1 states that the purpose of the law is to strengthen 'reconciliation and national stability, ensuring the supreme interest of the country, ending rivalries and building confidence among the belligerent parties'. The original proposal quotes both from the Prophet Muhammad sparing his defeated enemies as well as the reconciliation that occurred in South Africa and Tajikistan. The law announces an amnesty to embrace all factions from different stages of the conflict, and calls on members of the armed opposition to embrace reconciliation. In concept, the law is based on a 'thicker' reconciliation strategy. In addition, the law makes an association between Northern Alliance commanders in the Parliament and the Taliban, in the call for reconciliation.

The Amnesty Law should be reviewed in the context of the continuation of the presidential amnesty decrees of 2003[140] and 2005,[141] which pursued the objective to disarm, demobilise and reintegrate (DDR) the Taliban forces, provided they were not linked to alQaeda. However, this is a stark contrast to the National Action Plan on Peace, Justice and Reconciliation, which urged the establishment of a truth commission but with a prohibition against amnesties for international crimes, see below.[142] The direct cause of the adoption of the Amnesty Law is believed to have been the Human Rights Watch report *Blood-Stained Hands* on 6 July 2005,

---

137 The Amnesty Law.
138 Garth Meintjes and Juan Méndez, 'Reconciling Amnesties with Universal Jurisdiction', *International Law Forum*, 2 (2000), pp. 76–97, esp. p. 85.
139 *Ibid.*
140 On the 2003 amnesty see Rubin, 'Transitional Justice and Human Rights in Afghanistan', p. 567.
141 The 2005 amnesty was offered to rank and file Taliban members provided they were not linked to alQaeda or responsible for crimes against humanity. Nader Nadery said he worried that Taliban fighters and leaders brought in through the reconciliation process would claim immunity from future prosecution. Cited in N.C. Aizenman, *Washington Post* Foreign Service, 16 February 2005, p. A12.
142 *Peace, Reconciliation and Justice in Afghanistan*, Action Plan of the Government of the Islamic Republic of Afghanistan, 6–7 June 2005. See, further, Section 6.6.3.2.

publishing a list of persons accused of perpetrating civil atrocities committed during the 1992–96 civil war,[143] and the death sentence passed on Saddam Hussein by the Iraqi tribunal.

The original draft of the Amnesty Law launched by *Wolesi Jirga* (the lower house of Parliament) included a blanket amnesty to 'all the political wings and hostile parties who had been in conflict before the formation of the interim administration'.[144] President Karzai revised the bill, with the amendment that recognised the individual right of victims to seek justice and bring complaints against those who are alleged to have committed war crimes. The amendments are interesting; for example, the individual criminal liability for international crimes is not completely blocked by the amnesty, although the enforcement of criminal justice is placed in the victim's hands. On the other hand, such a restriction may not affect the jurisdiction of international courts or a third state acting under universal criminal jurisdiction.

As to its subject matter, the Amnesty Law applies to the international core crimes, *i.e.* genocide, crimes against humanity and war crimes. According to the Action Plan, and also according to Islamic law, such international core crimes must not be subject to an amnesty:

> The importance of 'reconciliation' (key action 4) is particularly recognised because durable peace requires social re-integration and reconciliation in this country. Measures should be taken to make possible the return and re-integration of all hostile groups in the society and lead to the reduction of tensions, warmongering and bloodshed in the country. This peace and justice perspective cannot mean to excuse genocide, war crimes, crimes against humanity and other gross violations of human rights. On the contrary, bold action against these crimes is itself a universally accepted moral principle. (...) The commission of such crimes does not fall into the scope of amnesty on the basis of the principles of the sacred religion of Islam and internationally accepted standards.[145]

Thus, importantly, a complete exemption from prosecutions or punishment would contradict the previous national practice. In

---

143 *Blood-Stained Hands: Past Atrocities in Kabul and Afghanistan's Legacy of Impunity* (New York: Human Rights Watch, 6 July 2005).

144 Amnesty draft 2007.

145 *Ibid.*

addition, Afghanistan, by the ratification of the ICC Statute in 2003, has affirmed the duty under international law to prosecute core international crimes. The evaluation of the subject matter of the Amnesty Law is, however, even more complex. This is due to the fact that the law refers to acts limited to political offences, and as such the subject of a more lenient treatment, and in addition may be limited to the belligerent parties.

As to the temporal scope of application, the Amnesty Law under Article 3 para. 1 applies to crimes committed before the establishment of the interim administration. However, under Article 3 para. 2, the amnesty is extended to those 'who are still in opposition to the Islamic Republic of Afghanistan and cease enmity after the enforcement of this resolution and join the process of national reconciliation, and respect the Constitution and other laws and abide [by] them'. The Amnesty Law thereby facilitates an open-ended continued commission of amnesty for crimes committed after the Bonn Agreement in 2001 and, even more controversially, crimes committed after the ratification of the ICC statue in 2003. The United Nations Commissioner for Human Rights in 2010 called for the repeal of the controversial law, which at present serves only the purpose of shielding alleged war criminals from prosecution.[146]

6.6.4 Steps towards accountability and reconciliation

6.6.64.1 The action plan
Based on the findings of the public consultations, the AIHRC presented the President with the 'Peace, Reconciliation and Justice Action Plan' in June 2005 in an international conference in The Hague.[147] The plan comprised a comprehensive transitional justice strategy. The action plan was launched to address human rights

---

146 'It's [a] global UN position not just specific to Afghanistan. [A] blanket amnesty is our problem, I think, for very obvious reasons,' Norah Niland, the Afghanistan representative of the UN High Commissioner for Human Rights said. 'For a country to move out of a crisis it needs to be able to deal with the past', she told a news conference in Kabul. 'So the amnesty law is a real concern because of the blanket amnesty.' And further: '...the UN High Commission for Human Rights, Afghan civil society, human rights NGOs in and outside the country have asked that the law be repealed.' UN News Centre, 25 March 2010.
147 The Action Plan for Peace, Reconciliation, and Justice, 2005.

violations and war crimes committed by various warring parties from the Soviet occupation of 1979 to the fall of the Taliban in late 2001. The plan covers a full range of processes and mechanisms associated with Afghanistan's attempts to address past abuses. The action plan comprised five key areas: (1) a symbolic commitment to remember, and aid the recovery of, victims of past abuses; (2) institutional reforms including the vetting of governmental officials; (3) truth-seeking and documentation; (4) reconciliation; and (5) strategies for criminal justice. The plan also includes the return and reintegration of perpetrators of minor offences, of hostile groups into society, and the reduction of tensions and bloodshed. The plan lacks details and definite commitments, but it includes a strong statement against amnesty for genocide, war crimes, crimes against humanity and other gross violations of human rights. The plan states that 'considering the clear Koran verses and the international law, no amnesty should be provided for war crimes, crimes against humanity and other gross violations of human rights'.

President Karzai passed the Action Plan in December 2005. However, the plan has still not been implemented, and the time limit for implementation has been exceeded. The enactment of the amnesty before any disclosure of the past has taken place severely damages the criteria of good faith. Other reconciliation measures have since been adopted, although without any immediate success.[148]

Semple, in a recent study, suggests that the lack of sustained commitment to reconciliation on the part of the Afghan government and its Western backers is the major reason why opportunities for reconciliation have been wasted. In a three-year period between 2004 and 2007, he conducted interviews with some two hundred Afghans, who were involved directly or indirectly in the country's insurgency. The study discloses that:

---

148 The Musa Qula Accord: The Accord signed in September 2006 drew on traditional Afghan institutions for reconciliation. However, a lack of strategy and coherence from the government to support the administration led to its collapse. The Peace Jirga hosted in Kabul in July 2007 with a large delegation of Pakistani Pashto was successful, but failed to facilitate a link to a genuine process for reconciliation. See also Mohammad Masoom Stancekzai, *Thwarting Afghanistan's Insurgency. A Pragmatic Approach towards Peace and Reconciliation.* Special Report 212 (Washington, DC: United States Institute of Peace Press, 2008).

[The] government's structures, the Western military and political presence, and the United Nations were all singularly ill equipped and often
disinclined to take the needed steps to enable the Afghans to reconcile
and reintegrate peacefully back into society. The collective failure of those
engaged in the political process in Afghanistan since 2001 to develop
credible alternatives for these men and those like them, has led to pro-
found consequences. A disastrous escalation of the conflict increased [the]
questioning of the basis of international engagement in Afghanistan and
a loss of hope that the fall of the Taliban regime might mark the return of
peace to Afghanistan.[149]

The UN Security Council sanctions list includes 142 Taliban fig-
ures. Out of this list, only 12 have been reconciled and reintegrated
into public life in Afghanistan. On the other hand, the official
Strengthening Peace Program by the end of 2007 claimed to have
reconciled 4,634 former combatants. However, it is a subject of
intense debate as to which part of the population they come from,
or whether these individuals are of strategic significance. After
2005, top-level reconciliation of Taliban almost disappeared. As
argued by Semple:

> In modeling the Taliban and their influence, it is perhaps easier to
> describe what they are not. They are not simply a terrorist organisation,
> a tribal movement, or a modern party. They are in the vanguard in the
> sense that they assert moral authority over the general population, and
> they are a brotherhood in the sense that they have a strong awareness of
> identity and solidarity.[150]

The intrinsic power balance of synchronised reconciliation is thus
missing.

6.6.5 The restorative option: A linchpin for legal culture and traditional justice?

In the intervening time, a search for alternative resolutions rests
within traditional local institutions of dispute settlement in

149 Semple, *Reconciliation in Afghanistan*, p. 5.
150 *Ibid.*

Afghanistan known as *jirgas* and *shuras*. They address issues ranging from negligible bodily harm and agricultural conflicts to serious and sometimes violent conflicts. They utilise various dispute settlement mechanisms.[151] Because Afghanistan's formal justice system lacks human and material resources and common legitimacy, the powers of these local traditional institutions are increased. The two systems could ideally complement each other to deliver justice efficiently, in accordance with Afghan legal norms and international human rights principles. There are aspects of *jirgas/shuras* that suggest their utility relative to formal justice institutions. *Jirgas/shuras* are shown in empirical studies to be slightly more accessible, more efficient, less corrupt, and more trusted by Afghans when compared with formal state courts.[152] The study implies that decisions of *jirgas/shuras* are accepted more easily as binding, compared with decisions made by the state courts. Rarely, the decisions need to be enforced. On the other hand, in the same survey, Afghan citizens preferred in the case of serious crimes to bring the case before state courts and regarded these institutions as more effective in delivering justice, promoting human rights and other international standards.[153] A serious concern for the stakeholders is that settlements made by *jirgas/shuras* may violate Afghan secular laws and international obligations. Women are excluded from participating in the decision-making of *jirgas/shuras*, resulting in serious consequences for their status and the protection of their rights. The local councils also issue *hudud* sentences[154] and operate without the guarantees of a due process, because they are not formally connected to the secular laws or to the laws of *sharia*.

151 For a comprehensive study, see *The Customary Laws of Afghanistan* (New York/Kabul: International Law Foundation, September 2004).

152 Afghan Human Development Report, *Bridging Modernity and Tradition: Rule of Law and the Search for Justice*, 2007, pp. 95–96.

153 *Afghan Perceptions on the Rule of Law: A Citizens' Survey*, conducted by the Afghan Center for Socio-Economic and Opinion Research (ACSOR) Surveys and commissioned by the (Afghan) Center for Policy and Human Development (CPHD), January–February 2007.

154 The *hudud* crimes are considered crimes against God. They are prescribed and defined by God and may not be modified by men. *Hudud* literally means limit or restriction. *Hudud* forms the bounds of acceptable behaviour. Crimes classified as *hudud* are the most severe and carry harsh punishments. See *e.g.* Mansour, 'Hudud Crimes', in C. Bassiouni (ed.), *The Islamic Criminal Justice System* (London: Oceana Publications, 1982).

6.6.6 Summary of the case of Afghanistan

The need for establishing accountability measures, and a 'thicker' reconciliation, is urgent. So far, the self-amnesty law is the only measure. When not connected with any non-judicial measures, the result is impunity. The national consultations show that this process contradicts the public view. Striking the right balance will ultimately depend on having to correspond to the will of the people. For instance, as stated by the Afghan Independent Human Rights Commission: 'No mechanisms it could suggest will truly bring justice and start to heal the pain and suffering of the people unless [they are] based on the will and desires of the people.'[155]

The United Nations High Commissioner for Human Rights, Navi Pillay, in her 2009 speech to the Security Council on the protection of civilians in armed conflict and the situation in Afghanistan, summarised the failure: 'The failure to pursue a credible transitional justice strategy, including holding to account those responsible for the gravest of crimes over more than three decades of war and the climate of impunity created thereby, is a significant factor in the political turmoil and growing insecurity that now envelop Afghanistan.'[156] She concludes on the pressing need to 'close the gap' between policy and practice, and emphasised both accountability measures and victims' redress: 'Closing that gap will require a greater commitment by all to the explicit application of international law, and to its enforcement (...) And it will require an unwavering focus on the three, mutually reinforcing, imperatives of accountability for perpetrators, redress for victims and protection for the vulnerable.'[157]

PART IV FINAL REMARKS

International legal standards play a critical role in enabling post-conflict societies to make the change from a culture of impunity to accountability. In this context, clear and predictable obligations for the states to enforce criminal justice are the unequalled guarantees for avoiding a policy-based justice and impunity. However, as the

---

155 The Afghan Independent Human Rights Commission, *A Call for Justice*, 2005.
156 United Nations Security Council, Statement of Navi Pillay, United Nations
       High Commissioner for Human Rights, New York, 11 November 2009.
157 *Ibid.*

discussion has shown, the interest of justice may be in conflict with peace.[158] The principled contradictions between retribution and restoration are, to some extent, replaced by the interests of restoring justice in a widely perceived way. Also, preferably, they complement rather than contradict each other. Thus, a flexible approach and imaginative combinations may have a better chance to accomplish the ambitious goals of the transition: justice, peace and democratic authenticity. The text has revealed the advantages of using restorative elements to enhance the transition and contribute to a balance between the anti-impunity paradigm and the circumstances and exigencies of the individual state.

However, there are requirements of minimum standards of a genuinely reconciliatory process. For the most serious crimes and the perpetrators most responsible, there is a clear presumption against amnesties. The normative pull of the justice element, particularly a duty to prosecute and the rights of the victims, remains crucial. For instance, the outcome of the Gacaca courts of Rwanda relies on a multifaceted hybrid structure, with the ICTR as a guarantee for not refraining from the limitations for the core crimes. Orentlicher stated that:

> International legal norms affirming that atrocious crimes ought to be punished have provided a powerful antidote to impunity. While there are of course times when those same norms cannot be enforced, it has seemed preferable to say 'not yet' than to reframe global norms in terms that suggest prosecuting atrocious crimes is nothing more than an option. For if we were to move entirely away from the language of legal obligation, we would take from those operating on the frontlines of their countries' struggle for decency one of the most potent weapons in their arsenal.[159]

The admissibility of amnesties should thus be the topic of both an objective evaluation of the gravity of the crimes, and a subjective evaluation of the good faith and genuineness of the state. There is, however, a remarkable difference between the 'close the door to the past' arguments in favour of 'impunity' amnesties, and a sincere

---

158 Ambos, 'The Legal Framework of Transitional Justice', para. 3.
159 Orentlicher, 'Settling Accounts Revisited', p. 22.

restoration. The latter will face both the past and the future, and include the victims' redress and the societies' need for social repair by disclosure of the truth.

While carefully taking into account these considerations and demands, restorative elements may be constructive especially for the inclusion of traditional dispute mechanisms and legal culture. A skilful use could bridge the gap between the standards of international law and the 'imperfect justice' in the post-conflict scenarios. Additionally, the principle of complementarity as laid down in the ICC Statute may embrace the national states' use of traditional dispute mechanisms, which by their natures aim at reconciling the parties. The Court has not yet decided upon these distinctions.

The case of Afghanistan shows the complex and intertwined relationships between justice and peace. So far, in the opinion of this author, the attempted solution of overcoming the past by the unconditional renunciation of criminal justice is endangering the peace in Afghanistan. The Afghan procedures have failed to end the 'bad relations', and violence and conflicts recur. Indeed, the Amnesty Law has not displayed reconciliatory effects at any recognisable levels. The Afghan case suggests that restorative elements can only be *complements* in the transitional scenarios, and that the reconciliatory effects of criminal justice should not be underestimated.

References

Alexy, R., *Theorie der Grundrechte* (Baden-Baden: Nomos, 1985).

Alvarez, J., 'Crimes of the State/ Crimes of Hate: Lessons from Rwanda', *Yale Journal of International Law*, 24 (1999), pp. 365–484.

Ambos, K., 'The Legal Framework of Transitional Justice: A Systematic Study with a Special Focus on the Role of the ICC' in K. Ambos, J. Large, and M. Wierda (eds.), *Building a Future on Peace and Justice: Studies in Transitional Justice, Peace and Development* (Berlin: Springer, 2010).

The Colombian Peace Process and the Principle of Complementarity of the International Criminal Court: An Inductive, Situation-based Approach (Berlin: Springer, 2010).

Annan, K., cited in Charles Villa-Vicencio, 'Why Perpetrators Should Not Always be Prosecuted: Where the International Criminal Court and Truth Commissions Meet', *Emory Law Journal*, 49 (2000).

Baines, E.K., 'The Haunting of Alice: Local Approaches to Justice and Reconciliation in Northern Uganda', *International Journal of Transitional Justice*, 1 (1) (2007), pp. 91–114.

Bassiouni, M.C., (ed.), 'Introduction' in *Post-Conflict Justice* (Ardsley, NY: Transnational Publishers Inc., 2002).

Bassiouni, M.C. et al., *An Assessment of the Justice Sector and Rule of Law Reform in Afghanistan and the Need for a Comprehensive Plan.* Paper prepared for the Rome Conference, 'The Rule of Law in Afghanistan,' 2–3 July 2007.

Bell, C., 'The New Law of Transitional Justice' in K. Ambos, J. Large, and M. Wierda (eds.), *Building a Future on Peace and Justice: Studies in Transitional Justice, Peace and Development* (Berlin: Springer, 2010), pp. 105–27.

Benzing, M., 'The Complementarity Regime of the International Criminal Court: International Criminal Justice between State Sovereignty and the Fight against Impunity,' in A. von Bogdandy and R. Wolfrum (eds.), *Max Planck Yearbook of United Nations Law*, Vol. 7 (Leiden: Koninklijke Brill N.V., 2003), pp. 591–632.

Bergsmo, M., and Kruger, P., 'Observers' Notes' (Article by Article), in Otto Triffterer (ed.), *Commentary on the Rome Statute of the International Criminal Court* (Munich: Beck, Hart, Nomos, 2008).

Bolton, J.R., 'The Risks and Weaknesses of the International Criminal Court', *Law and Contemporary Problems*, 64 (2001), pp. 167–180.

Boraine, A., *A Country Unmasked: Inside South Africa's Truth and Reconciliation Commission* (Oxford University Press, 2001).

Buergenthal, T., 'The United Nations Truth Commission for El Salvador', *Vanderbilt Journal of Transnational Law*, 27 (3) (1994), pp. 497–544.

Cassese, A., *International Criminal Law* (Oxford University Press, 2008).

Combs, N.A., *Guilty Pleas in International Criminal Law: Constructing a Restorative Approach* (Palo Alto, CA: Stanford University Press, 2007).

Corey, A., and Joireman, S.F., 'Retributive Justice: The Gacaca Courts in Rwanda', *African Affairs*, 103 (2004), pp. 73–89.

Crocker, D.A., 'Reckoning with Past Wrongs: A Normative Framework', *Ethics & International Affairs*, 13 (1) (1999), pp. 43–64.

Daly, E., 'Between Punitive and Restorative Justice. The Gacaca Courts in Rwanda', *N.Y.U. Journal of International Law and Politics*, 34 (2002), p. 355.

Daly, E., and Sarkin, J., *Reconciliation in Divided Societies: Finding Common Ground*, Pennsylvania Studies in Human Rights (Philadelphia: University of Pennsylvania Press, 2007).

Des Forges, A., *Leave None to Tell the Story: Genocide in Rwanda* (New York: Human Rights Watch, 1999).

Dorronsoro, G., 'The Security Council and the Afghan Conflict', in V. Lowe, A. Roberts, J. Welsh and D. Zaum (eds.), *The United Nations Security Council and War: The Evolution of Thought and Practice since 1945* (Oxford University Press, 2008).

Drumbl, M.A., 'Law and Atrocity: Settling Accounts in Rwanda', *Ohio Northern University Law Review* 31 (2005), Rev. 41.

Dugard, J., 'Possible Conflicts of Jurisdiction with Truth Commissions', in Antonio Cassese, Paola Gaeta and John R.W.D. Jones (eds.), *The Rome Statue of the International Criminal Court* (Oxford University Press, 2002).

Elster, J., 'Justice, Truth, Peace', in Morten Bergsmo and Pablo Kalmanovitz (eds.), *Law in Peace Negotiations* FICHL Publication Series No. 5 (Peace Research Institute Oslo (PRIO) 2009), pp. 21–28.

Fletcher, L.E., and Weinstein, H.M., 'Violence and Social Repair: Rethinking the Contribution of Justice to Reconciliation', *Human Rights Quarterly*, (2002), pp. 573–639.

Galtung, J., in Mohammed Abu-Nimer (ed.), *Reconciliation, Justice and Co-existence in Theory and Practice* (Lanham, MD: Lexington Books, 2001).

Gavron, J., 'Amnesties in the Light of Development of International Law and the Establishment of the International Criminal Court', *International and Comparative Law Quarterly*, 51 (2002), pp. 93–95.

Harper, J., 'The Gacaca Experiment: Rwanda's Restorative Dispute Resolution Response to the 1994 Genocide,' *Pepperdine Dispute Resolution Law Journal*, 1 (2005).

Hayner, P.B., *Unspeakable Truths: Facing the Challenge of Truth Commissions* (New York: Routledge, 2002).

'Truth Commissions: A Schematic Overview', *International Review of the Red Cross*, 88 (862) (2006), pp. 295–310.

Ignatieff, M., 'Articles of Faith', *Index on Censorship*, 5 (1996), pp. 110–22.

Kerber, G., 'Overcoming Violence and Pursuing Justice: An Introduction to Restorative Justice Procedures', *The Ecumenical Review*, 55 (2) (April 2003), pp. 151–57.

Kirkby, C., 'Rwanda's *Gacaca* Courts: A Preliminary Critique', *Journal of African Law*, 50 (2) (2006), pp. 94–117.

Kiza, E., Rathgeber, C., and Rohne H.-C., *Victims of War: An Empirical Study on War-Victimization and Victims' Attitudes towards Addressing Atrocities* (Hamburg: Hamburger Institut für Sozialforschung, 2006) Hamburger edition online, available at http://www.his-online.de (last accessed 19 September 2010).

Kress, C., and Grover L., 'International criminal law restraints in peace talks to end armed conflicts of a non-international character' in Morten Bergsmo and Pablo Kalmanovitz (eds.), *Law in Peace Negotiations* FICHL Publication Series No. 5 (Peace Research Institute Oslo [PRIO] 2009), pp. 29–53.

Kritz, N.J., 'Where We Are and How We Got Here: An Overview of the Developments in the Search for Justice and Reconciliation' in Alice Henkin (ed.), *The Legacy of Abuse: Confronting the Past, Facing the Future* (Washington, DC: The Aspen Institute, 2002).

Lederach, J.-P., *Building Peace: Sustainable Reconciliation in Divided Societies* (Washington, DC: United States Institute of Peace Press, 1997).

Lerche, C., 'Peace Building Through Reconciliation', *The International Journal of Peace Studies*, 5 (2) (2000).

Llewellyn, J., and Howse R., 'Institutions for Restorative Justice: The South African Truth and Reconciliation Commission', *University of Toronto Law Journal*, 49 (3) (1999), pp. 355–388.

Lutz, E., and Reiger, C., *Prosecuting Heads of State* (Cambridge University Press, 2009).

Maley, W., *The Afghanistan Wars*, 2nd edition (London: Palgrave Macmillan, 2009).

Mallinder, L., *Amnesty, Human Rights and Political Transition* (Oxford: Hart Publishing, 2008).

Mani, R., 'Reparation as a Component of Transitional Justice in the Aftermath of a Violent Conflict: Pursuing "Reparative Justice" in the Aftermath of Violent Conflicts' in K. de Feyter, S. Parmentier et al. (eds.), *Out of the Ashes* (Antwerp: Intersentia, 2005), pp. 53–82.

Mansour, A.A., 'Hudud Crimes', in C. Bassiouni (ed.), *The Islamic Criminal Justice System* (London: Oceana Publications, 1982).

Meintjes, G., and Méndez, J., 'Reconciling Amnesties with Universal Jurisdiction', *International Law Forum*, 2 (2000), pp. 76–97.

Méndez, J.E., 'Accountability for Past Abuses', *Human Rights Quarterly*, 19 (2) (1997), pp. 255–82.

Minow, M., *Between Vengeance and Forgiveness: Facing History after Genocide and Mass Violence* (Boston: Beacon Press, 1998).

Moreno Ocampo, L., Chief
Prosecutor of the International
Criminal Court, in K. Ambos,
J. Large, and M. Wierda (eds.),
*Building a Future on Peace and
Justice: Studies in Transitional
Justice, Peace and Development*
(Berlin: Springer, 2010).

Møse, E., cited in Francois-Xavier
Nsanzuwera, 'The ICTR
Contribution to National
Reconciliation', *Journal of
International Criminal Justice*, 3
(4) (2005), pp. 944–49.

Orakhelashvili, A., *Peremptory Norms
in International Law* (Oxford
University Press, 2006).

Orentlicher, D., 'Settling Accounts
Revisited: Reconciling Global
Norms with Local Agency',
*The International Journal of
Transitional Justice*, 1 (2007),
pp. 10–22.

O'Shea, A., *Amnesty for Crimes in
International Law and Practice*
(The Hague: Kluwer, 2002).

Robinson, D., 'Serving the
Interest of Justice: Amnesties,
Truth Commissions and the
International Criminal Court',
*European Journal of International
Law*, (2003), pp. 481–505.

Roche, D., 'Truth Commission
Amnesties and the International
Criminal Court', *British Journal
of Criminology*, 45 (2005), pp.
565–596.

Roht-Arriaza, N., 'The New
Landscape of Transitional
Justice' in N. Roht-Arriaza (ed.),
*Transitional Justice in the Twenty-
First Century: Beyond Truth versus
Justice* (Cambridge University
Press, 2006).

Rubin, B.R., 'Transitional
Justice and Human Rights in
Afghanistan', *International
Affairs*, 79 (3) (2003), pp. 567–81.

Sarkin, J., *Carrots and Sticks: The TRC
and the South African Amnesty Process*
(Antwerp: Intersentia, 2004).

Sarkin, J., and Daly E., 'Too Many
Questions, Too Few Answers.
Reconciliation in Transitional
Societies', *Columbia Human
Rights Law Review*, 35 (2004), pp.
661–728.

Schabas, W.A., 'Amnesty, the Sierra
Leone Truth and Reconciliation
Commission and the Special
Court for Sierra Leone', 11 *UC
Davis Journal of International Law
and Policy* 145 (2004).

'Genocide Trials and *Gacaca*
Courts', *Journal of International
Criminal Justice* 3 (2005),
pp. 879–95.

Seibert-Fohr, A., 'The Relevance
of the Rome Statutes of the
International Criminal Court
for Amnesties and Truth
Commissions', in A. von
Bogdandy and R. Wolfrum (eds.),
*Max Planck Yearbook of United
Nations Law*, Vol. 7 (Leiden:
Koninklijke Brill N.V., 2003),
pp. 553–90.

*Prosecuting Serious Human Rights
Violations* (Oxford University
Press, 2009).

Semple, M., *Reconciliation in
Afghanistan* (Washington, DC:
United States Institute of Peace
Press, 2009).

Sharf, M., 'The Amnesty Exception
to the Jurisdiction of the
International Criminal Court',
Cornell International Law Journal,
32 (1999), pp. 507–527.

Stahn, C., 'Complementarity, Amnesties and Alternative Forms of Justice: Some Interpretative Guidelines for the International Criminal Court', *Journal of International Criminal Justice*, 3 (2005), pp. 695–720.

Stancekzai, M.M., *Thwarting Afghanistan's Insurgency. A Pragmatic Approach towards Peace and Reconciliation*. Special Report 212 (Washington, DC: United States Institute of Peace Press, 2008).

Suhrke, A., and Borchgrevink, K., 'Negotiating Justice Sector Reform in Afghanistan', *Crime, Law and Social Change*, 51 (2) (2009), pp. 211–30.

Sullivan, D., and Tiffs, L., (eds.), *Handbook for Restorative Justice: A Global Perspective* (London: Routledge, 2006).

Tadjbakhsh, S., and Schoiswohl, M., 'Playing with Fire? The International Community's Democratization Experiment in Afghanistan', *International Peacekeeping*, 15 (2) (2008), pp. 252–67.

Teitel, R., *Transitional Justice* (Oxford University Press, 2000).

Tutu, D., *No Future without Forgiveness* (London: Rider, 1999).

'Reflections on Moral Accountability', *International Journal of Transitional Justice*, 1 (1) (2007), pp. 6–7.

Van den Herik, L.J., *The Contribution of the Rwanda Tribunal to the Development of International Law* (Leiden: Martinus Nijhoff Publishers, 2005).

Van Zyl, P., and Freeman, M., 'Conference Report' in Alice H. Henkin (ed.), *The Legacy of Abuse: Confronting the Past, Facing the Future* (Washington, DC: The Aspen Institute, 2002).

Wardak, A., 'Jirga: Power and traditional conflict resolution in Afghanistan', in John Strawson (ed.), *Law after Ground Zero* (London: Routledge Cavendish, 2002), pp. 187–204.

Werle, G., *Principles of International Criminal Law* (The Hague: TMC Asser, 2005).

Williams, S., 'Amnesties in International Law: The Experience of the Special Court of Sierra Leone', *Human Rights Law Review*, 5 (2005).

Selected documents

ICC Office of the Prosecutor, *Paper on some policy issues before the Office of the Prosecutor*, September 2003.

ICC Office of the Prosecutor, *Report on Prosecutorial Strategy*, 14 September 2006.

ICC Office of the Prosecutor, *Policy Paper on the Interest of Justice*, September 2007.

The Joinet Report, E/CN.4/ Sub 1997/20/Rev. 1, 2 October 1997.

UN Security Council, The Rule of Law and Transitional Justice in Conflict and Post-Conflict Societies. Report of the Secretary-General. S/2004/616, 23 August 2004.

UN–ECOSOC Commission on Human Rights, Promotion and Protection of Human Rights. Impunity, 27 February 2004.

Updated set of principles for the protection and promotion of human rights through actions to combat impunity, E/CN.4/2005/102/Add. 1, 8 February 2005.

UN DOC, A/HCR/12/18, 6 August 2009, *Annual Report of the United Nations High Commissioner for Human Rights* (...), 'Analytical Study on Human Rights and Transitional Justice'.

Selected documents on Afghanistan

Agreement on Provisional Arrangements in Afghanistan Pending the Re-establishment of Permanent Government Institutions, also known as the *Bonn Agreement* after the location of its signature. Doc.s/2001/1154 of 5 December 2001.

Blood-Stained Hands: Past Atrocities in Kabul and Afghanistan's Legacy of Impunity (New York: Human Rights Watch, 6 July 2005).

Reconciliation and Justice in Afghanistan, Action Plan of the Government of the Islamic Republic of Afghanistan, 6–7 June 2005.

The Afghan Independent Human Rights Commission, *A Call for Justice* (Kabul: AIHRC, 2005).

The Customary Laws of Afghanistan

(New York/Kabul: International Law Foundation, September 2004).

Afghan Human Development Report 2007, *Bridging Modernity and Tradition: Rule of Law and the Search for Justice.*

Afghan Perceptions on the Rule of Law: A Citizens' Survey, conducted by the Afghan Center for Socio-Economic and Opinion Research (ACSOR) Surveys and commissioned by the (Afghan) Center for Policy and Human Development (CPHD), January–February 2007.

Amnesty, National Reconciliation and Stability Law entered into force with its publication December 2009 in the Official Gazette No. 965.

Selected table of cases

ICJ *Arrest Warrant,* of 11 April 2000 (*Democratic Republic of Congo* v. *Belgium*) Judgment of 14 February 2002, ICJ Reports 2002.

ICC, *Prosecutor* v. *Lubanga Dyilo*, Decision concerning Pre-Trial Chamber I's Decision of 10 February 2006 and the

Incorporation of Documents into the Record of the Case against Mr Thomas Lubanga Dyilo, ICC-01/04-01706. 24 February 2006.

SCSL, *Prosecutor* v. *Morris Kallon*, Brima Bazzy Kamara, SCSL-2004-15-PT-060-I, SCSL-2004-15-PT-060-II, Appeal Chamber (13 March 2004).

ICTY, *Prosecutor* v. *Furundzija*, No. IT-95-17/1-T, Judgment of the Trial Chamber, 10 December 1998.

ECHR, *Hugh Jordan* v. *UK* Judgment 4 May 2001.

IACHR, *The Barrios Altos* case, Inter-American Court of Human Rights, 14 March 2001.

South African Constitutional Court, *Azanian Peoples Organization (AZAPO)* v. *The President of the Republic of South Africa and others*, 1996, 4(SA).

Colombia Constitutional Court, *Gustavo Gallon Giraldo y otros*. Judgment of the Justice and Peace Law, Sentencia No. C370/2006, 18 May 2006.

List of Contributors

ELIZABETH BAUMANN is a judge in Stavanger City Court, with previous work experience as a prosecutor and barrister. From 2006–2007, she was a judge mentor for Afghan judges in the Central Narcotic Tribunal in Kabul, and from 2008–2011, she was a PhD. candidate, at the Faculty of Law, University of Bergen, related to her project 'States in transition and the duty to prosecute international crimes, with lessons from Afghanistan.' She defended her dissertation in December of 2011. Her research interests lie in the interface between transitional justice and international criminal law, with a particular interest in peace processes.

INGUN FORNES is a research fellow at the Faculty of Law, University of Bergen. Her field of interest is the criminal justice system and especially the juvenile justice system. Previous she has been a legal advisor to the Committee on juvenile delinquency (NOU 2008: 15).

KATJA JANSEN FREDRIKSEN is a PhD fellow at the Faculty of Law, University of Bergen and holds a Master of Arts in Arabic languages and culture from the University of Leiden, the Netherlands. Her current research comprises comparative studies between Islamic and Norwegian family law, while her master thesis focused on border disputes between Yemen and Saudi Arabia.

EIRIK HOVDEN is a PhD student at the Institute of Archaeology, History, Cultural Studies and Religion, University of Bergen. He is currently doing research on Islamic (Zaydi) public trusts (waqf) and jurisprudence and legal history in Yemen.

LINDA GRÖNING is assistant professor at the Faculty of Law, University of Bergen. Her fields of interest are criminal law, EU law and legal theory and she has published several books and articles within these fields. Her doctorate thesis, *EU, staten och rätten att straffa: Problem och principer för EU:s straffrättsliga lagstiftning* (in English: *EU, the State and the Right to Punish: Problems and Principles for EU Legislation*), provides a legitimacy analysis of the evolving legislative penal competence at the EU level. She is currently working on a post doc project on the principled structure of the criminal justice system. Gröning is project leader for the research project *Functionality in the Criminal Justice System* and together with Jørn Jacobsen, for the project *Theory in Practice: Risks and Responses in Modern Criminal Law*.

JØRN JACOBSEN is currently post. doc.-researcher at the Faculty of Law, University of Bergen. His field of interest is criminal law and legal theory. He has published several books and articles on these subjects. His ph.d.-thesis, *Fragment til forståing av den rettsstatlege strafferetten* (in English: *Fragments concerning the criminal law in the democratic Rechtsstaat*), discussed the aims and limits of criminal law within a democratic *Rechtsstaat*. His is currently working on a project concerning the concept of crime. Jacobsen is project leader for the research projects *Criminal Law Theory – A New Norwegian Approach*, and, together with Linda Gröning, *Theory in Practice: Risks and Responses in Modern Criminal Law*.

HENDRIK KAPTEIN is an associate professor of jurisprudence and philosophy of law at Leiden University. He studied (legal) philosophy at the University of Amsterdam. His doctoral dissertation is about moral argumentation and its foundations. He also wrote and edited books (in Dutch and in English) on legal ethics, evidence and proof, restorative justice and related subjects. His academic articles and media activities also cover argumentation and general legal practice subjects. He is active in university administration and as a member of non-profit organization boards as well.

DAVID C. VOGT has a Master's Degree in Philosophy from the University of Bergen. His main academic interests are legal and moral philosophy, criminal law and restorative justice. He has also worked on issues of aboriginal justice, conflict resolution and rhetoric.

Other books of interest for the reader

ISBN: 978-91-7359-025-9
392 pages in hard cover
Language: Swedish

Linda Gröning

EU, staten och rätten att straffa

Problem och principer för EU:s straffrättsliga lagstiftning
(*EU, the State and the Right to Punish: Problems and Principles for EU Legislation*)

Kan straffrätten regleras på EU-nivå, delvis fristående från staten, och ändå vara legitim? Eller annorlunda uttryckt: Har EU rätt att straffa, på vilka grunder och inom vilka gränser?

(Is it possible to regulate criminal law at EU level, keep it partly independent of the state, and still be legitimate? Or put differently: Does the EU have the right to punish, on what grounds and to what extent?)

ISBN: 978-91-7335-029-7
454 pages in hard cover
Language: Swedish

Fredrik Van Kesbeeck Andersson

Försäkringsfusk

Tillvägagångssätt, straffansvar och försäkringsutredning
(*Insurance fraud: Modi operandi, criminal liability and insurance investigations*)

Bokens tre avsnitt belyser var och en företeelsen försäkringsfusk. Tillsammans bildar de en enhet som visar problematiken kring de motstående intressen som finns i försäkringsförhållanden mellan å ena sidan försäkringsgivaren och å den andra försäkringstagaren.

(The book's three sections each highlight insurance fraud. Together they form a unit that shows the problem of the conflicting interests that exist in the insurance relationship between the insurer and the insured.)

www.santerus.se